What Readers are Saying

"Scripturally, a believer can be a vegetarian or a meat eater and be obedient to God's word ... *Holy Cow!* points those who are beginning to ask, 'What does God tell me to eat?' to the Holy Scriptures for the answers."

>   Dr. Gordon S. Tessler,
>   Author of *The Genesis Diet*

"... This book will help you understand one of the most misunderstood subjects in the Bible. Every believer should read it—with an open mind."

>   Dr. Richard Booker,
>   Author of *The Mystery of the Scarlet Thread*,
>   Founder of the Institute for Hebraic-Christian Studies

"Your publication is a fine, stimulating, and magnificent work on a topic many Christians refuse to think about. Thank you for your courage to discuss the crucial topic of eating from the biblical perspective. I wholeheartedly endorse *Holy Cow!* It is hard to express in a few words the depth of your study. I strongly recommend this superb book for all who want to advance in their daily walk with the Lord."

>   Jiri Moskala, Th.D. Ph.D.
>   Professor of Old Testament Exegesis and Theology
>   Andrews University

"This simple-to-understand book uses basic hermeneutic principles to properly interpret what the Bible says about eating meat... Egan is clear that our diets are not a salvation issue, while at the same time encouraging obedience to God's Word. I highly recommend this much-needed book."

>   Robin Sampson
>   Author of *A Family Guide to theBiblical Holidays* and
>   *The Heart of Wisdom Teaching Approach: A Guide to Biblical Education*

"… Displaying a keen intellect, respect for traditional interpretations, and a refreshing zeal for understanding and living by every word of God, Hope makes an excellent case for rethinking traditional Christian views on this subject. May it lead us all to a closer relationship with our Lord and Savior."

>David Treybig
>Pastor
>Church of God, a Worldwide Association

"*Holy Cow!* is winsome and full of grace! Hope Egan provides a great balance of logic and humor on this very important issue."

>Sue Gregg,
>*The Busy Woman's Guide to Healthy Eating*,
>International speaker and teacher

"I have found *Holy Cow!* to be a breath of fresh air. I greatly appreciate Hope Egan's inquisitive style of writing, which is sensitive to the needs of a wide variety of people, particularly Christians investigating their Hebraic roots."

>J. K. McKee
>Editor, TNN Online

"This book should come with a warning. If you read this book you may be leaving pork ribs and lobster off your personal menu. It is that thought provoking and biblically convincing."

>Jackson Crum
>Lead Pastor
>Park Community Church

"This is the type of book that will make any student of the Bible happy. The author clearly and carefully leads readers through a penetrating and fascinating study of God's Word. Yet her style of writing is conversational, never confrontational. It's a perfect mix of enthusiasm and exhortation!"

>Joyce Handzo
>ChristianBookPreviews.com

"As a pastor in a mainline protestant congregation who keeps a biblically ordained diet, I often feel like a stranger in a strange land. Many in the Church do not fully understand the biblical/kosher lifestyle, and so I often find myself teaching them. This book has been a vital resource to me by helping me explain what the Bible says about our dietary choices and the fact that God really does care about what we eat."

> Bill Beyer
> Pastor
> Trinity English Lutheran Church

"*Holy Cow!* will help you see the menu plan for dinner with clearer focus and greater blessing. This well-written book brings peace of mind as you recognize God's protection for us even in our food choices."

> Annette Reeder
> Biblical Nutrition Consultant
> Author, Consultant, Speaker

"*Holy Cow!* presents a clear picture of what the disciples said about food in the New Testament and how that pertains to the Torah's dietary instructions. This question seems to be arising more and more in Christendom today. For anyone who wants balanced, well-researched information on this subject, do not hesitate to pick up a copy of this book!"

> Beth Holland
> Author, Speaker and Bible Teacher

"What's important about this book is that Egan doesn't force a right-or-wrong debate about eating meat or following kosher rules. Instead, she simply represents both biblical and scientific thoughts about why God gave those specific dietary rules in Leviticus and asks us to consider how they apply to our lives today."

> Joanne Brokaw
> Freelance writer and columnist

HOLY COW!

DOES GOD CARE ABOUT WHAT WE EAT?

HOPE EGAN

HOLY COW!

DOES GOD CARE ABOUT WHAT WE EAT?

HOPE EGAN

Heart of Wisdom Publishing
Copyright © 2012 by Hope Egan. All rights reserved.
Publication rights Hope Egan.

Author grants permission to reference short quotations (less than 400 words) in reviews, magazines, newspapers, Web sites, or other publications. Requests for permission to reproduce more than 400 words can be made directly to the author.

The material contained in *Man Alive! There's More!* is based upon First Fruits of Zion's *Torah Club Volume Four* and *Torah Club Volume Five* and is reprinted here with permission from D. Thomas Lancaster.

First Edition, April 2005
Second Printing, October 2005 (revised)
Third Printing, October 2007 (revised)
Fourth Printing, December 2009
Second edition, October 2012

Printed in the United States of America

Catalogue Information: CBA Category Information: CLV/CLF/DHE
ISBN: 978-0-9819407-1-7

Unless otherwise noted, Scripture quotations taken from the New American Standard Bible®, Copyright © 1960, 1962, 1963, 1968, 1971, 1972, 1973, 1975, 1977, 1995 by The Lockman Foundation. Used by permission. (www.Lockman.org) Throughout this publication the name "Christ" is rendered "Messiah."

Cover Design: Avner Wolff

ATTENTION CHURCHES, SYNAGOGUES, STUDY GROUPS, TEACHERS AND OTHER ORGANIZATIONS: Quantity discounts are available on bulk purchases of this book for educational, fundraising or gift purposes, or as premiums for increasing magazine subscriptions or renewals. Special books or book excerpts can also be created to fit specific needs. For more information, please contact the publisher.

Heart of Wisdom

200 Coble Road, Shelbyville, TN 37160
www.HeartOfWisdom.com
info@heartofwisdom.com

*To God, from whom all blessings flow,
and to my husband Brian: my best friend,
faith partner and a whole lot more.*

Acknowledgments

So many people contributed to *Holy Cow!*'s first edition, as well as to my ruminations since then, that they are too many to name.

The bottom line is that this book would not be without the initial and continued blessing of First Fruits of Zion, *Holy Cow!*'s original publisher. Many thanks to them, especially *mensch* extraordinaire D. Thomas Lancaster, who "bequeathed" the rights to his "Man Alive! There's More!" section to me. I'm also grateful for their willingness to create this second edition, camera ready for the new publisher.

As I updated parts of this edition, I drew on several experts, including D. Thomas Lancaster, Aaron Eby (author of *Biblically Kosher: A Messianic Jewish Perspective on Kashrut*), Tim Hegg (of TorahResource.com) and Temple Grandin (world-renowned expert on cattle slaughter). I am also grateful to Rick Spurlock who was a helpful sounding board during the process, and to Debbie and Heidi Barrett for their editing help.

Finally, I am grateful to my sweet, amazing, wonderful husband and best friend Brian for his continued love and support, and to my family, friends and colleagues who made the original work possible.

Hope Egan
October 2012

Contents

Acknowledgments	vii

Foreword to the First Edition
  by Dr. Rex Russell, author of
  What the Bible Says about Healthy Living Preface
	xi

Foreword to the Second Edition
  by By Jordan S. Rubin
  Founder and CEO of Beyond Organic
	xiii

Preface	xv
Part I: Hope's Perspective	1
Prologue Lunch with a Nice Jewish Girl	3
1 In the Beginning Food and the Hebrew Scriptures	11
2 Did God Flip a Coin? Scientific Support for the Biblical Food Laws	29
3 What Would Jesus Eat? First-Century Judaism's Historical Background	39

4 The New Testament View
  Reconciling Apparent Contradictions
  with the Hebrew Scriptures
	49

5 Avoiding Blood, Fat and Things Strangled Is *Kosher* Meat the Answer?	61
6 Meat and Milk Did My Ancestors Take it Too Far?	77

7 Conclusion God's Word Does Not Change—and Neither Does the Physiology of Pork	83
Epilogue Second Edition Update	89

Part II: Man Alive! There's More!   93

Appendices   133

Bible and Apocrypha Passages	135
List of Clean and Unclean Animals	141
Resources	147
Bibliography	149
Scripture Reference Index	151
Subject Index	155

Foreword to the First Edition

By Dr. Rex Russell

Author of *What the Bible Says about Healthy Living*

Hope Egan has an important message for the Christian community: God cares about what we eat.

Affirming what I have discovered from my 30 years of study on this topic, *Holy Cow!* has been a tremendous encouragement to me.

First, this well-written book, which reads like a novel, testifies to God's powerful Spirit. What else could explain the identical conclusions drawn by me (a 60-something, life-long Christian doctor from Arkansas) and a 30-something Midwestern Jewish girl, who met Jesus only a few years ago?

Second, it's a pleasure to see the list of "evangelists" for God's design for healthy eating grow. Hope joins Gordon Tessler, Jordan Rubin, Don Colbert, Joyce Rogers, Reginald Cherry, myself and others to spread the wisdom contained in God's instruction manual. Sure, insights are revealed in other approaches to eating. However, people who live their lives "by the Book" would do well to seek God's perspective on this topic, especially as it relates to meat. As our voices continue to grow, we will collectively impact our world's growing health crises. I have personally experienced radical health benefits from aligning my food choices with God's Word. My arthritis, acne and chronic abscesses (carbuncles) disappeared—within a month of letting go of pork, shellfish, blood and hard animal fats. These are all foods that the Bible urges us to avoid. (Giving up my favorite foods wasn't easy; during my "last supper" of shrimp I downed 47 of them!)

Finally, I am excited to find a book that addresses biblical meat eating as thoroughly as Hope Egan and D. Thomas Lancaster have. As an author and speaker, I continually answer questions about the Hebrew Scriptures' meat laws and their applicability to Christians. *Holy Cow!* is an invaluable resource, one that I certainly recommend to others.

May God bless you as you pursue God's wisdom for eating.

Rex Russell, MD
April 2005

Foreword to the Second Edition

By Jordan S. Rubin
Founder and CEO of Beyond Organic

I first met Hope Egan in 2004, shortly after my book *The Maker's Diet* was released. After hearing me speak to a large group of health and wellness professionals in Wheaton, Illinois, she approached me and asked if I would endorse her new book, *Holy Cow! Does God Care about What We Eat?*

"Does God care about what we eat?" This question was posed to me nearly a decade earlier when I was suffering from multiple "incurable," illnesses. After studying Scripture, history and science, I have concluded that God absolutely cares about what we eat and created wonderful foods to nourish (or in my case restore) our bodies.

Upon conquering my illnesses through application of a biblically-based diet and lifestyle program, I dedicated my life to helping transform the health of God's people, one life at a time. I also had a dream to one day produce the biblically inspired foods that made such a big difference in my health. After a quick read of Hope's manuscript for *Holy Cow!*, I agreed that Hope made a compelling presentation on God's plan for our diet, especially where meat is concerned, so I was proud to endorse the work.

Fast forward to 2012.

I am blessed to have achieved my dream and am now producing what I believe to be some of the world's healthiest foods and beverages, including biblically raised and processed beef. Upon learning about my farming project, Hope contacted me again, this time to ask about the slaughter process our cattle go through before they are prepared for sale. "I am looking for resources for people who want to buy meat that has been raised *and* processed in a biblical manner," she told me.

My new company, Beyond Organic, provides consumers with grass-fed and finished cattle, slaughtered in accordance with the biblical principles Hope outlines in chapter 5: we thoroughly drain the animals' blood using kosher slaughter methods and state-of-the-art kosher equipment; we do not use the fat surrounding the lungs and the kidneys; and we do not process animals that have died by natural causes or been killed by other animals.

As Hope and I spoke, we realized how similar our journeys and frustrations about the nuances of biblical meat-eating were. Stunning. Shackling. Restraining systems. Topics neither of us had ever heard about suddenly became important as each of us endeavored to understand how the meat-related passages in the Bible could be applied today.

Wanting to neither blindly accept nor quickly reject the wisdom that our Hebrew ancestors had accumulated in their thousands of years of applying these verses, each of us arrived at similar conclusions, as Hope carefully outlines in the pages that follow.

For believers who are interested in honoring God with their entire being, body, soul and spirit, *Holy Cow!* will be an eye-opening read. Part testimony, part Bible study, it is an intelligent, entertaining walk on the Bible's path to healthy eating.

> Jordan S. Rubin
> October 2012

Preface

In 1996 I began to entertain a belief contrary to my Jewish friends and family: that Jesus is the promised Messiah.[1]

What was I thinking? That Jesus is *not* the Messiah is a belief deeply entrenched in my family history. Was I really qualified to reevaluate this? How could I veer off the path that my forefathers had walked for thousands of years?

After struggling with these questions for several months, I realized that the generations before me probably had not approached the "Jesus question" as intentionally as I was trying to. I didn't know any family members who read the Hebrew Scriptures (Old Testament) in which the Messiah is foreshadowed, let alone study the New Testament to see if Jesus fit the bill. Instead, most of them—consciously or unconsciously—inherited their rejection of Jesus from their parents, grandparents and rabbis.

A little knowledge of history reinforced their view. During the Crusades, Jews were slaughtered in Jesus' name. During the Spanish Inquisition, "Convert to Christianity or die" was the theme. During the Reformation, Martin Luther called for believers to destroy Jewish synagogues and religious books. Although I was ignorant of this history, my inherited rejection of Jesus was solidified by television evangelist scandals and seeing crosses burned at Ku Klux Klan rallies. These people appeared to be Jesus' most visible representatives, so I wanted nothing to do with Him.

What Softened My Stance?

While recovering from a series of personal trials, I was encouraged by friends to pray for strength and wisdom. Desperate, I dabbled in prayer, and within a few days I sensed that the God of my ancestors was indeed still alive and well. Unable to ignore His existence, I set out to learn more about Him. But where to start?

It was Christians who seemed most interested in talking about God. These people focused on growing, changing, learning and healing—with God at the center of their lives. But the thought of becoming a "Christian" seemed strange. How could I make that leap when I knew nothing about Jesus? I realized how strongly held my disbelief was, yet how little analysis I had done. As an educated, intelligent businesswoman, I reckoned that it was time to start.

In spite of my (real or imagined) family opposition, I braved the journey with an open mind as best I could. Discovering information about Jesus that contradicted my core beliefs disturbed me, but it eventually produced fruit in every area of my life—beyond my wildest expectations. Had I not ventured outside of my preconceived theology and my ancestors' belief system, I would have missed it.

Now, I invite you to embark on a similar journey of open-minded exploration. The implications might scare you, but consider suspending the beliefs you've inherited from your family, your teachers and our society. At the very least, I invite you to become aware of the lenses with which you read the Bible. What assumptions or beliefs—conscious or unconscious—influence your interpretations? Where did they come from? How do they line up with the original, historical context in which the Bible was written?

As you explore, it may feel strange to consider new perspectives on familiar Bible passages. However, if you approach this process prayerfully and thoughtfully, it may be one of the most invigorating studies you've ever undertaken.

Endnotes

[1] The word "messiah" comes from the Hebrew word *moshiach*, which means "anointed one." In the Greek, *moshiach* is translated *Christos*, which is often translated into English as "Christ." Most Jewish folks, myself included, grow up believing that "Christ" is Jesus' last name (or a swear word) rather than an affirmation of His messiahship. As such, I like to refer to Jesus as "Messiah" rather than "Christ."

Part I
Hope's Perspective

Prologue
Lunch with a Nice Jewish Girl

"Does the split pea soup have ham in it?" Elizabeth asked the waiter. After he answered and took our order, I asked her, "Are you a vegetarian?"

"No," she casually said, "I'm just trying to keep *kosher*."

"*Kosher*?" I asked her. "You mean you have two sets of dishes? And you don't eat milk and meat together?"

"No," Elizabeth answered, "I don't keep traditions that require two sets of silverware and dishes; those aren't in the Bible. I focus on the biblical ones, like not eating pork or shellfish. Leviticus 11 spells out pretty clearly which foods God created to be eaten and which ones He didn't. I don't believe that He changes His mind, so I try to follow His guidelines."

"Hmmm …"

I first met Elizabeth at our church's book club. I was excited to have lunch with her, since her wisdom and passion about the Bible were apparent, and since, like me, she was a Jewish believer in Jesus. The concept of avoiding pork and shellfish, however, seemed peculiar. At this point I had been a follower of Jesus for several years and never considered that any faith-based eating guidelines might apply to me. I was under the distinct impression that God did not care about what we ate.

Dietary Law Confusion

From my childhood I knew that observant Jews don't eat pork or shellfish. In addition, they avoid eating dairy and meat together, and they don't eat meat-based foods on dishes used for dairy foods (and vice versa). I was open to anything God wanted for me, but did He really care whether I ate today's beef chili in yesterday's cereal bowl? Before making any radical changes for God, I would need to believe that it was truly His will and completely in line with His Word. From my reading, the meat/dairy separation currently practiced in observant Jewish homes was not found in the Bible.

While Elizabeth's perspective on "keeping *kosher*" was much simpler than mine, it was still odd. After all, I'd never heard any Christians even mention abstaining from pork. I certainly didn't abstain. Ribs were my favorite meal and my choice for my annual birthday dinner. Besides, wasn't ham a traditional Christian holiday food? If faithful Christians celebrated Jesus' birth and resurrection with pork, I figured they must have carefully weighed this decision—especially since the Hebrew Scriptures (Old Testament) contains explicit prohibitions against it.[1]

Yet Elizabeth's avoidance of pork intrigued me.

Is the Bible Reliable?

My lunch with Liz raised an issue that had troubled me for several years. I had often wondered, "How can I rely on the New Testament to learn about Jesus, when it sometimes seemed to contradict my ancestors' Scriptures?"[2]

Five years earlier I had joined a small Christian faith community in which I learned about Jesus and the Bible—two things I knew very little about. I eventually committed my life to Jesus, but my journey was filled with confusion. Why did Jesus have to die? What's the atonement? Is Satan real?

Whenever I asked questions, my friends always turned to the Bible as the ultimate information source. Their reverence for this book seemed extreme, but their wise ways of dealing with life's toughest issues hooked me. Since the Bible was the foundation for that wisdom, I was compelled to read it.

My first reaction to the Christian Bible was shock: I had no idea that over two-thirds of it was identical to the Jewish Bible. How could Christianity share such a large chunk of its Scriptures with Judaism, yet the two religions seem so different?

I started at the beginning. As I read, I rediscovered characters from my brief religious education: Adam and Eve, Noah, Joseph and other familiar heroes. My Bible was coming alive with the same stories that I had glossed over as a child.

Leaning heavily on my footnotes, I read about vaguely recognizable people and events with both joy and confusion. Growing up, I didn't really believe in God, yet our family observed Passover much like Exodus 12 directs. I was excited to see the ancient roots of my family's tradition, but why didn't my new Bible friends even mention Passover? As I continued to read, the questions continued to surface. Deuteronomy 6 commands us to mark the doorposts of our houses with God's Word to remind us of Him. Again, this is something we did growing up; why is it totally absent in Christianity? Leviticus 11 plainly forbids us to eat pork. So why did most Bible-believing Christians eat it?

Sadly, I didn't really care about Jewish faith observances, since they felt empty to me growing up. I was, however, confused. I needed to understand why some commands in the Hebrew Scriptures seemed to be ignored if I was going to take the Bible and Christianity seriously. I yearned for a worldview that made sense, but being urged to believe in the truth of the whole Bible—while disregarding emphatic parts of it—literally made me queasy.

When I asked why we omitted certain Bible passages from our daily lives, my friends gave me confident, authoritative answers like, "Jesus fulfilled the Law" and "We are no longer under Law; we're under grace." Still perplexed, I assumed that my young faith kept me from understanding their answers and trusted that concepts I didn't fully grasp would become clear later. After all, I wasn't stupid. I graduated from the University of Illinois with highest honors, passed the CPA exam on my first try, and counseled senior executives on how to plan for their financial futures. I gave up trying to reconcile the apparent contradictions and committed to "sit in the tension," knowing that God would eventually put the pieces together for me. I continued on my Christian journey, eating my special rib dinners and leaving the doctrinal issues to the theologians.

I thought I had let go of the whole contradiction issue, but after my lunch with Elizabeth, my questions reappeared. In addition, I realized that my last few rib dinners had grossed me out, and that I no longer enjoyed the shrimp and scallop meals that I'd occasionally cook. Was this the power of suggestion, or was the Holy Spirit moving and convicting me?

God's Design for Healthy Eating

At this point in my life, I was NOT looking to eliminate anything from my diet. For both physical and emotional health reasons I'd already spent many years striving to clean up my eating habits, and—only by God's grace—had been reasonably successful. In fact, it was only through my assorted food struggles that I realized how much I needed God and His power in my life. I couldn't have changed my diet without Him and His empowering Spirit.

Now, just when I finally felt at peace about how I was eating, and my physical and emotional health were restored, God showed me something else to let go of: ribs, one of my few lingering food indulgences. Oy!

Committed to doing God's will in all areas of my life, I took the plunge and gave up pork and shellfish. Since the other areas that I'd submitted to Him (like money, work and relationships) had always turned out beautifully, I trusted that the pork thing would too. Because of my skepticism, however, I needed to understand it—both biblically and scientifically.

A book by Dr. Gordon Tessler, a Christian nutrition expert, gave me a new perspective. His book, *The Genesis Diet*, began to help me see that God might very well care about what I ate. How? By illuminating God's design for eating, which includes both plant- and meat-based foods, but which excludes pork and shellfish. Even more importantly, *The Genesis Diet* challenged some common theology used to explain why the Hebrew Scriptures' instructions no longer apply. My brain-fog began to clear as I found answers to some of my most vexing questions.

Rejuvenated Faith

Besides learning about God's design for eating, I learned how to read and study the Bible more carefully. Until that point, I focused on listening to my teachers, studying commentaries, and reading footnotes rather than reading the Word itself. Another bonus from my exploration: a better understanding of the Bible's ancient Near Eastern setting. I knew that "context, context, context" was important for understanding the Bible, but few resources adequately shed light on this ancient culture.

In addition to reading *The Genesis Diet*, I began to read magazines and books published by First Fruits of Zion, TorahResource.com, and other messianic publishers. These writers unpack the Scriptures, using mainly the Bible itself, ancient texts and their knowledge of the original Greek and Hebrew. I always knew that Jesus was Jewish. Now I finally began to understand the holidays He celebrated, the foods He ate and the culture He lived in—and how these things applied to me. My two-dimensional faith was becoming three-dimensional!

I soon discovered an entire sub-culture within Christianity that believes that the Hebrew Scriptures' instructions apply to believers in Jesus as a natural response to their relationship with God—not as a prerequisite. They believe that Jesus is the Messiah, and that we are saved by grace, through faith (Ephesians 2:8). However, they also believe that Jesus "fulfilled the Law" by giving the Hebrew Scriptures its fullest meaning. How did He do this? By interpreting it properly and by fully living it out.[3]

Excited to reconcile some of my life's biggest faith questions, and finally feeling like I had found a theological home, I shared this information with my non-Jewish husband, Brian. He was understandably skeptical.

"You mean we're going to have to get two sets of dishes?"

Unfortunately, when he asked this question I was not as grounded as Elizabeth had been with me. My feeble response caused him to quote a flurry of Bible verses to prove that our existing food choices were perfectly in line with Scripture: "One person has faith that he may eat all things, but he who is weak eats vegetables only ... each person must be fully convinced in his own mind." (Romans 14:2, 5) "For everything created by God is good, and nothing is to be rejected if it is received with gratitude; for it is sanctified by means of the word of God and prayer." (1 Timothy 4:4–5) and "Eat anything that is sold in the meat market without asking questions for conscience' sake ..." (1 Corinthians 10:25)

Not knowing how to respond, I wept, and the tension between us grew. The more I tried to convince him that examining the historical context and original languages shed new light on this topic, the more verses he quoted, and the more convinced he became that

I was wrong. At one point he told me, "Languages-schmanguages! It's pretty clear to me that it doesn't matter what we eat!"

God had been the glue that bound us together, but now it felt like our different interpretations of His Word were driving a wedge between us. How crazy is that? We tried to ignore the issue, but I felt estranged from him. Distraught, I completely lost my appetite and struggled to eat, a rare occurrence for me.

Explaining my new perspective was not working, so I tried a subtler approach. I left my Hebraic roots of Christianity magazines lying around, hoping he would read one. It was inconceivable to Brian that this magazine, covered in Hebrew letters, could have anything to do with the Bible or Jesus. In fact, it filled him with dread. "Where is she going with all this? Is she going to become Orthodox? She's gone off the deep end—in a bad way."

Brian's antennae about my new studies went up quickly. He associated teachings that looked "Jewish" with the rejection of Jesus. While certainly not anti-Semitic (his love for me and my heritage was clear from the day I met him), he did fear that my current path was the first step towards abandoning Messiah. Since I had flirted with Orthodox Judaism earlier in my faith walk, his concerns were valid. There is no room in Orthodox Judaism for the messiahship of Jesus.

My husband had a passion for discerning truth from error, and he was very leery of anything not accepted by mainstream Christianity. He often listened to Bible teaching on the radio, and he was committed to using only trustworthy sources to help him understand God's Word.

To investigate the perceived "error" that I had slipped into, Brian picked up my latest magazine within a few weeks. The opening article affirmed how central Messiah is to our walk. The Passover-related articles pointed to Messiah. Most importantly, a featured article addressed the meat-related food laws of Leviticus 11 and many of Brian's original concerns.

After reading this article and researching the topic himself, he was also convinced that the Bible's instructions about which meats God designed to be eaten still applied to us. Concerned about why this new conclusion was so different from what he had always been taught, my heresy-hunting husband joined my path, and together we began our journey to reconcile the Old and

New Testaments and their current applicability to our lives. The foundation of faith on which we had originally built our marriage was not only restored, it has since grown and flourished with our shared view of the continuity of Scripture!

Join My Journey

Meanwhile, I continued to investigate God's design for healthy eating, which extends far beyond the issue of meat. Urged by others to share what I had been learning, I spoke about biblical eating at our church's women's ministry events and met Amy, who shared my passion for God and all of His intelligently designed foods. Together we started a monthly cooking club, spoke at local churches' women's events, and wrote a cookbook.[4]

During this time I dialogued with many women and heard their questions about God's design for eating. Some of these women shared my earlier confusion about pork and shellfish; others were blessed to find peace and clarity with traditional explanations. These conversations, in part, have inspired me to write this book.

Regardless of whether your current beliefs overlap with mine, I feel privileged that you've read this far and pray that you continue reading. If you do, please hold my perspective with an open hand. Why? Folks who suspend judgment often find this exercise fascinating, regardless of their ultimate conclusion.

God's perspective on food is not the core of my faith; it is merely a single facet in a lifelong journey of spiritual growth and discovery. I share this information with you so you can learn more about the specific topic at hand—not as a way to gain right-standing before God. This book is not about doing something (or avoiding something) so that we can have a relationship with Him or be "saved." Rather, exploring this topic is a response to our faith. It arises naturally from our longing for obedience to God. *Because* we already have a relationship with Him, we respond to His love for us by seeking His will and wisdom in all areas of our lives—including what we eat. As redeemed people, we bear the most fruit when we submit our whole selves to our Creator. In other words, dietary issues are not the core of my faith, but they are the main focus of this book.

Neither a theological treatise nor a diet manual, *Holy Cow!* is simply what I, a layperson, have learned as I have attempted to discern God's instructions for eating.[5] You may or may not agree with my conclusions, but I pray that this investigation enriches your understanding of the Bible and that you find great joy in the process!

Questions to discuss and ponder

1. What beliefs about Jesus have you inherited from your family, your religious educators or society? Which have you researched on your own? What has that research involved?
2. What beliefs about eating pork and shellfish have you inherited from your family, your religious educators or society? Which have you researched on your own? What has that research involved?
3. What do you hope to learn from this book?
4. What do you understand the term "keeping *kosher*" to mean?
5. Does God factor into any of your food choices? If so, how did you arrive at your conclusions?

Endnotes

[1] Leviticus 11:7 and Deuteronomy 14:8
[2] I share how I have begun to reconcile these apparent contradictions in chapter four.
[3] Traditional interpretation generally holds that because He "fulfilled the Law" we need not follow it. This is discussed further in chapter four.
[4] The *What the Bible Says about Healthy Living Cookbook: Simple and Tasty Recipes Featuring God's Ingredients* (Heart of Wisdom).
[5] See Part II, *Man Alive! There's More!*, written by Bible teacher D. Thomas Lancaster, for deeper, more theological explanations of my Part I material.

In the Beginning
Food and the Hebrew Scriptures

In the churches I have attended, "fellowship" is often synonymous with "eating," but I have rarely heard the topic of food addressed from the pulpit. When I hear it discussed on Christian radio, the teachers make it clear that God does not care about what we eat. They cite verses like Matthew 6:25, where Jesus tells His disciples not to worry about what to eat or drink. But is that possible? Could God really not have an opinion about an activity that every human being must do several times a day? Does the Bible address every aspect of life, including birth, death, marriage, sex, work and money, but forget this one?

I am convinced that God has a detailed plan for how we fuel our bodies. The psalmist seems to agree:

> He makes grass grow for the cattle, and plants for man to cultivate—bringing forth food from the earth …
>
> The lions roar for their prey and seek their food from God.
>
> There is the sea, vast and spacious, teeming with creatures beyond number—living things both large and small.
>
> These all look to you to give them their food at the proper time. When you give it to them, they gather it up; when you open your hand, they are satisfied with good things. (Psalm 104:14, 21, 25, 27–28)

If God is so thoughtful with the animals' food provisions, how much more so does He provide for us?

In the Beginning

Let's start at the beginning. Genesis chapter one gives us our first peek at God's design for what we eat. On the sixth day, after God created man and commanded him to be fruitful and multiply, He addressed one of our most basic needs: food.

> Then God said, "Behold, I have given you every plant yielding seed that is on the surface of all the earth, and every tree which has fruit yielding seed; it shall be food for you." (Genesis 1:29)

What do we learn from this simple verse?

Just as God deliberately created plants, animals and humans, He also intentionally designed what we would eat. From the beginning of time, fruits, vegetables, grains, beans, nuts and seeds were God's healthy staples for mankind. Because He cares for us and our nutritional needs, our loving Creator specifically designed food for us.

Examining seed-bearing plants reveals how well-devised God's plant-based foods are:

> Seeds seem almost too good to be true … A scientific examination of seeds indicates that they could not have developed by random chance. Their unique qualities point to the fact that they were designed by a benevolent Creator.[1]

Dr. Rex Russell (a Christian medical doctor) goes on to explain how seeds (which include grains, beans and nuts) grow everywhere in the world, in any climate, and reproduce quickly. They have a long storage life: Kernels found in Egyptian tombs can still be sprouted after 4,000 years. Nutritionally—if they are not processed or refined—these intelligently designed seeds meet nearly all of our nutritional needs, since they are filled with vitamins, minerals, fiber and even protein.

Here is another example. Most folks have heard that taking small amounts of aspirin helps prevent heart problems. The downside to taking aspirin, however, is that by ingesting it in medicinal form, it actually increases the risk of other problems, such as hemorrhagic strokes. God's perfect Genesis 1:29 food, on the other hand, is a win-win for the body:

> Apparently produce such as fruits and vegetables has just the right amount of aspirin to prevent both kinds of strokes—unnecessary clotting [which leads to heart attacks] and hemorrhagic strokes. Just three vegetables a day decrease the incidence of strokes and heart attacks by a significant amount.[2]

The myriad of disease-fighting, health-promoting foods found in Genesis 1:29 illustrate how God created our food using great detail.

In discerning God's plan for eating, some Christian vegetarians and vegans start and end with Genesis 1:29. (Vegetarians generally eat eggs and dairy products, while avoiding red meat, chicken and fish; vegans avoid all animal products.) To their credit, Genesis 1:29 foods are packed with life-giving nutrients that most Americans would do well to eat more of, especially since Genesis 2:9 repeats God's initial food design for mankind: "Out of the ground the LORD God caused to grow every tree that is pleasing to the sight and good for food." In fact, the prophet Daniel is practically a commercial for vegetarianism. Insisting on eating nothing but vegetables for ten days, he and his buddies appeared "better ... than all the youths who had been eating the king's choice food." (Daniel 1:15)

While plant foods contain far more protein than most folks realize, Genesis 1:29 foods do lack some nutrients that are only found in animals and animal products.[3] It is not surprising, then, that we see meat enter into mankind's diet. The biblical menu expands a few chapters later, when we meet Noah.

Noah

Most people have heard about Noah and the great flood that destroyed most of the earth's life forms. In preparation for the downpour, Noah took only two of each animal onto the ark with him, right? Wrong. God actually tells Noah:

> You shall take with you of every clean animal by sevens, a male and his female; and of the animals that are not clean two, a male and his female. (Genesis 7:2)

While God did tell Noah to take one pair of each unclean animal, Noah was actually told to collect *seven* pairs of the clean ones.

What can we discern from this obscure fact? The distinction between clean and unclean animals appeared long before the existence of the Jewish people or the laws of the Covenant. In fact, since the flood occurred nearly 1,000 years before the giving of the Law at Mount Sinai, the distinction between clean and unclean animals appears to have universal application. It is not just a Jewish thing. In both Jewish and Christian faith traditions, Noah (like Adam) represents all of mankind. In other words, the difference between clean and unclean animals seems relevant for everyone—non-Jewish and Jewish people alike.

Let's ponder this. First, how did Noah distinguish between clean and unclean? The laws detailing the distinctions (Leviticus 11) had not yet been given. But if he was to gather seven pairs of clean animals and only one pair of unclean, he must have known the difference. Perhaps since "Noah walked with God," (Genesis 6:9) additional, unrecorded conversations between them took place where God explained the distinctions. Or maybe (as some Jewish traditions hold) this knowledge was passed down from Adam, who named the animals and might have had this information.

Here is another question: Why did God require Noah to take seven pairs of clean animals but only one pair of unclean animals? Looking at post-flood events gives us some clues.

After enduring the flood, Noah eventually steps back onto dry ground. Just as God did with Adam in Genesis one, He first commands Noah to populate the earth (9:1). Just as with Adam, He then issues a new food-related directive:

> Every moving thing that is alive shall be food for you; I give all to you, as I gave the green plant. (Genesis 9:3)

God alludes to His earlier plant-based food plan (the green plant) and now provides man with animal sources of food. Let the meat eating begin!

But what did God mean by "every moving thing that is alive ..."? Was this open-season on every type of living creature, including skunks, rats and snakes? Probably not. More likely, Noah abstained from eating these and other animals that God classifies as unclean. (We will learn about clean and unclean meat later in this chapter.)

Think about it. Barely out of the gate of biblical history, we saw God give Adam "every seed bearing plant on the face of the earth" for food (Genesis 1:29). But we know that "every" plant did not really mean "all" plants. After all, some plants are toxic and therefore not fit for consumption. Also, in Genesis 2:16–17 God limits what Adam could eat, telling him that he is not to eat from the tree of the knowledge of good and evil. These food restrictions illustrate how—in spite of language that appears to be all-inclusive—the verse granting permission for Noah to eat "every moving thing" does not necessarily mean that God granted license to eat "all moving things."

What would happen if Noah, in a fit of hunger, spit-roasted a pig shortly after the Genesis 9:3 pronouncement? As we will see, pigs are unclean, so Noah sheltered only two of them from the flood. Therefore, eating one would have meant immediate extinction for the entire species. Similarly, in Genesis 8:20, Noah's first sacrifice included "every clean animal" and "every clean bird." Had Noah offered up a dog (which is unclean), man's best friend would have immediately disappeared from the earth.[4] Since Scripture tells us that Noah sacrificed only clean animals, he probably ate only clean ones, in spite of being given "every moving thing" to eat. The New Living Translation seems to agree. Its paraphrase of Genesis 7:2 instructs Noah to "take along seven pairs of each animal *that I have approved for eating* and for sacrifice ..." (emphasis mine) Somehow Noah knew the difference and avoided eating and sacrificing the unclean ones.

Meat Eating after Noah

Several centuries after Noah, another universal figure of faith is introduced: Abraham. Throughout the book of Genesis, Abraham and his offspring are frequently seen tending to their herds and flocks.[5] In the Hebrew Scriptures, the Hebrew word translated as "herds" always refers to cows,[6] while the word for "flocks" generally refers to sheep, goats and lambs.[7] As we will soon see, the Hebrew Scriptures classify these animals as clean. At one point (Genesis 18) we see Abraham serve a choice calf to his heavenly guests.

Eventually Abraham begets Isaac, who begets Jacob (also named Israel), whose 12 sons become the 12 Tribes of Israel. Joseph (one of Jacob's sons) rises to fame in Egypt, where he eventually relocates his entire family. After a short-lived era of prosperity, Jacob's descendants become enslaved to the Egyptians for over 400 years.

God eventually delivers the Children of Israel from Egyptian bondage. In addition to Jacob's blood relatives, however, non-Hebrews (a "mixed multitude") and clean animals join in the escape from Egypt and the journey to Mount Sinai:

> Now the sons of Israel journeyed from Rameses to Succoth, about six hundred thousand men on foot, aside from children. A mixed multitude also went up with them, along with flocks and herds, a very large number of livestock. (Exodus 12:37–38)

Several weeks after the Exodus, God joins Israel (composed of the freed Hebrew slaves and the mixed multitude that accompanied them) in a covenant relationship at Mount Sinai. Having been redeemed from slavery, the Israelites are now blessed with godly instructions for living: God's Law, or *Torah* in Hebrew.

What, Exactly, Is the Torah?

The food laws related to meat are found in a part of the Bible called the *Torah*, the first five books of the Bible: Genesis, Exodus, Leviticus, Numbers and Deuteronomy. It is commonly referred to as the *Pentateuch* (based on the Greek word for the number five) or the Five Books of Moses, since Moses is considered the writer of these books. These writings include historical narratives, important genealogies, prophecies, beautiful poetry and God's laws for living. The rest of Scripture—both Old and New Testaments—is built on the Torah's foundation. It was the first piece of our Bible. For centuries, it was the whole Bible.

The Hebrew word *Torah* is better translated "instruction" than "law." The Rabbis often point out that if the Torah were merely the law of the Jewish people, it would not start with Genesis, which includes the story of Adam and Eve, the story of Noah and the story of the patriarchs. The natural conclusion? The Torah is much more than a legal code, and it applies to all of mankind—not just the Jewish people.

In the Hebrew Scriptures, God encouraged Joshua to meditate on and follow the Torah day and night;[8] the prophets called wayward Israel back to the Torah;[9] and David spoke passionately about reading and living out the Torah.[10] In New Testament times, the Torah was the cornerstone on which first-century Jews built their lives. Jesus affirms that the Torah is eternal;[11] Paul reminds Timothy that all Scripture (which at that time consisted of only the Hebrew Scriptures) is "God-breathed and useful for teaching, rebuking, correcting and training in righteousness,"[12] and James, the brother of Jesus, proclaimed that the Torah is perfect and gives freedom.[13]

Most importantly, Jesus lived out the Torah. In order to be sinless, He had to live His life in perfect accordance with His Father's commandments. If He failed to do so, He would have failed to be a sinless, atoning sacrifice. This is important to understand, since it means that the Torah will teach us a lot about Jesus. It teaches us how He lived, how He dressed,[14] how He worshipped;[15] it even teaches us what He ate. When we study the Torah, we study the Bible Jesus studied—and lived out.

What Were the Purposes of the Torah?

Most Christians rightly understand that one purpose of the Torah is to lead us to Messiah. In Galatians, Paul tells us that the Torah is like a tutor that leads us to Jesus.[16] How does it do that?

First, our Redeemer is woven into every aspect of the Torah. From the Garden of Eden to the Passover story to the sacrificial system, the Torah reveals different aspects of the Messiah.[17] He is essentially the main character in the story.

Second, God's standards for living—and the consequences of falling short of them as prescribed by the Bible—force us to look for a savior who will reconcile us to Him. We need someone to accept the harsh consequence of sin, since "the soul who sins will die," (Ezekiel 18:4) and "the wages of sin is death." (Romans 6:23) Knowing that we will always fall short, we are grateful that Jesus was willing to accept on our behalf the Torah's prescribed penalty for breaking God's commands. In addition, we look to a savior to supernaturally help us walk in God's ways. In our own strength, we cannot keep the Torah. We are slaves to our sin. Thankfully, through faith in Jesus' death and resurrection we are set free from the bondage of sin. His Spirit provides us with strength to live out God's commandments:

> I will give you a new heart and put a new spirit within you; and I will remove the heart of stone from your flesh and give you a heart of flesh. I will put My Spirit within you and cause you to walk in My statutes, and you will be careful to observe My ordinances. (Ezekiel 36:26–27)

With God's Spirit within us, we long to do His will, as revealed in His Word. King David, a man after God's heart,[18] provides us with a glimpse of how a redeemed heart naturally longs for the holiness provided by God's wise laws (*Torah*) and commandments:

> Give me understanding, that I may observe Your law [*Torah*] and keep it with all my heart. (Psalm 119:34)
>
> I shall delight in Your commandments, which I love. (Psalm 119:47)
>
> O how I love Your law [*Torah*]! It is my meditation all the day. (Psalm 119:97)
>
> Therefore I love Your commandments above gold, yes, above fine gold. (Psalm 119:127)

Did Torah Justify God's People?

The Torah is more than just a tutor to lead us to Messiah. According to Deuteronomy, following God's instructions glorifies God and allows Israel to reflect God to the nations.[19] When the other nations see God's people living according to His wise commandments, they will be envious for Israel's relationship with God.

Therefore, keeping Torah was designed to be a national-level witnessing tool.

As an added bonus, walking in the Torah's commands ultimately led to Israel's good health. For example, wisdom about avoiding corpses (Numbers 19:11) and disposing of human excrement (Deuteronomy 23:12–13) contributed to the people of Israel living "a lifestyle that kept them free from illness and plagues throughout history."[20] Following the Bible's food guidelines also likely contributed to their well-being. This is not surprising, given verses like Deuteronomy 4:40:

> … keep His statutes and His commandments which I am giving you today, that it may go well with you and with your children after you, and that you may live long on the land which the LORD your God is giving you for all time.

One thing the Torah never did was earn people their salvation. Some Christians believe that before Jesus came, the Law was used to justify people before God. That is to say that by keeping the Torah, people earned their relationship with God. But Scripture itself—both the New Testament and the Old—tells us that following the Torah never led to salvation. Right-standing with God has always come solely through faith in God's promises.[21]

Rather than following the Torah as a condition to be redeemed, people who were *already* redeemed received the Torah. Think about it. The Hebrew slaves were hopelessly caught in Egyptian bondage, unable to free themselves. First, God delivers them from Pharaoh's clutches. Then He brings them through the cleansing waters of the Red Sea. Only then, *after* they are delivered, does He give them the Torah. It is not as if God told the children of Israel, "If you keep my Torah, then I will redeem you from Egypt."

In the first verse of the Ten Commandments, God reminds His people that He has already delivered them from bondage: "I am the LORD your God, who brought you out of the land of Egypt, out of the house of slavery." (Exodus 20:2) Obedience to God's will flows from a spirit of gratitude—not from a quest for acceptance. Similarly, as God prepares to outline His instructions for His people, He gently reminds them who He is and what He's done for them. This reminds them how much He cares for them, and hints that His commandments are wise guidelines for living, not burdensome rules and regulations. The Ten Commandments were not given as the ten steps to salvation; they were given to a people already redeemed.[22] Living as God instructs us is—and has always been—a response to His grace.

To Whom Did God Give the Torah?

Normally we associate the Torah with the Jewish people. But in Exodus 12:37–38, we saw that a mixed multitude left Egypt with the Hebrew slaves and were part of the community that received the Torah at Mount Sinai. This means the Torah was given to both Jews and non-Jews alike. The Torah itself affirms this:

> As for the assembly, there shall be one statute for you and for the alien who sojourns with you, a perpetual statute throughout your generations; as you are, so shall the alien be before the LORD. There is to be one law and one ordinance for you and for the alien who sojourns with you. (Numbers 15:15–16)[23]

This passage amazes me! First, according to God's Word, non-Jews are welcome within Israel: no requirements are given other than having faith in the God of Israel. Second, God's laws apply to both Jews and non-Jews. Third, the Torah's application is "perpetual." It does not say "until Messiah comes" or any other qualification. Perpetual. Forever.

Now that we have a better idea what the Torah is (wise guidelines for living the life of faith out of love for God), and what it is not (a method for gaining God's acceptance), let's look at the most detailed food-related instructions in the whole Bible. They appear in Leviticus chapter 11 and again in Deuteronomy 14:3–20. If you are not well-versed with these passages, I strongly suggest that you read them before continuing. (The Appendix contains Leviticus 11.)

Food Laws or Sacrificial System Laws?

A quick skim of Leviticus 11 convinces many Christians that its contents are obsolete, since it is filled with sacrificial system lingo and plopped in the middle of several chapters about the sacrificial system. It takes new lenses to see this chapter differently. As we take a closer look, keep in mind that laws specific to the sacrificial system do not currently apply, since there is no Temple in Jerusalem.[24]

Also, remember that the Torah contains God's instructions for His redeemed people—not burdensome hurdles to jump over in order to be in relationship with Him.

Finally, keep in mind that Christianity often carves the Torah's commands into three broad divisions: moral, civil and ceremonial. Believers sometimes use this division to explain why we skip over many of the Torah's laws, assuming that the "civil" and "ceremonial" no longer apply.

Obviously we cannot follow all of the Torah's laws today. For example, some were given specifically to the high priest; some can only be followed if a Temple in Jerusalem exists; some are superseded by the laws of our land (where stoning our neighbor is not legal).[25] However, I think that the traditional three-fold division oversimplifies this situation. Perhaps it is time to revisit our God-given instruction manual and look at it anew.

For example, Leviticus 19 illustrates how much God's laws overlap and intertwine:

- Respect your parents (19:3)
- Observe the Sabbath (19:3)
- Don't worship idols (19:4)
- Fellowship offering guidelines (19:5–8)
- Leave part of your harvest for the poor (19:9–10)
- Do not steal (19:11)

Does the presence of the sacrificial system guidelines in 19:5–8 negate the commands around them? I do not think so.[26] Similarly, Leviticus 11 contains commands that both can be applied today (like food-related ones) and those that cannot (like sacrificial system ones). As in Leviticus 19, the presence of sacrificial system commands (that only apply when there's a Tabernacle/Temple) should not discourage us from considering the food-related ones:

> This is the law regarding the animal and the bird, and every living thing that moves in the waters and everything

that swarms on the earth, to make a distinction between the unclean and the clean [sacrificial system-related], and between the edible creature and the creature which is not to be eaten [food-related]. (Leviticus 11:46–47)

What's on God's Menu?

In the simplest terms, God provides "clean" animals to man for eating. Those deemed "unclean" were not to be eaten.

Man Alive! There's More!
Read about the difference between "clean" and "unclean" on pages 97–101.

Here is a brief overview of these guidelines; I will elaborate on each group's anatomy and physiology in the next chapter.

MAMMALS (Leviticus 11:3–8): God gives two parameters for eating mammals. To qualify for food, they must have a "split hoof" and must "chew the cud." For those of you who live in glass-and-steel cities, these terms have little meaning. Split hooves means that the animal's feet are entirely wrapped with a hard covering that is fully split, from front to back. Chewing the cud is a complex digestion process. Animals that chew their cud (known as "ruminants") have several stomachs that food passes through before being excreted. The next chapter expounds on this process. Animals who qualify as ruminants include cows, sheep and goats. Pigs, which have split hooves, do not qualify, because they do not chew their cud.[27]

FISH (Leviticus 11:9–12): According to Leviticus 11:9, fish eligible to be considered food must have fins and scales. Heart-healthy favorites like salmon, halibut, tuna, mahi-mahi, flounder, sole, anchovies, cod, bass, grouper, haddock, perch, snapper, sardines and trout all qualify. It excludes scavengers, like shellfish (shrimp, lobster, oysters, clams), catfish and shark.

BIRDS (Leviticus 11:13–19): In contrast to mammals and fish, God's Word does not provide distinguishing characteristics for clean birds. Rather, it lists examples of unclean birds. As with fish, those listed—such as vultures and buzzards—are generally scavengers that God designed for purposes other than to be eaten.

Commonly eaten poultry, like chicken, turkey and duck, are not listed as unclean and are therefore considered clean.

INSECTS (Leviticus 11:20–23): Given John the Baptist's famous diet of locusts and honey,[28] it is not surprising to see locusts, grasshoppers and crickets on the menu. All other insects are not.

Most of Leviticus 11 speaks directly about food. Words like "you are not to eat" (11:4) and "you may eat" (11:3, 9) are clear directives about which animals God created to be food for us. These straightforward verses move beyond Genesis one, seven and nine and reveal more of God's food plan for mankind.

Detesting Unclean Meat

The Bible's dietary guidelines include some pretty strong language about deviations from God's menu. For example, the words "detestable" and "abhorrent" describe eating off-limits seafood:

> These you may eat, whatever is in the water: all that have fins and scales, those in the water, in the seas or in the rivers, you may eat. But whatever is in the seas and in the rivers that does not have fins and scales among all the teeming life of the water, and among all the living creatures that are in the water, they are *detestable* things to you, and they shall be *abhorrent* to you; you may not eat of their flesh, and their carcasses you shall *detest*. Whatever in the water does not have fins and scales is *abhorrent* to you. (Leviticus 11:9–12, emphasis mine)

To further emphasize how unsavory eating unclean meat is, Deuteronomy 14:3 re-introduces this topic by reminding the Israelites, "You shall not eat any detestable thing." In this verse, the Hebrew word translated as "detestable" is used elsewhere in the Torah to describe actions like child sacrifice (Deuteronomy 18:10–12). Similarly, God sees *eating* shellfish (and other unclean animals) as detestable—not the animals themselves or the people eating them. God created all animals, and He deemed them all to be good.[29] Just imagine a Cocker Spaniel puppy: snuggling with one is precious—but in our culture eating one seems detestable.

While we might agree that God has not changed His mind about child sacrifice, many Christians believe that He has shifted gears with these food guidelines. Has God changed His mind?

Holy Cow!

In the next chapter, we look at the scientific support for the biblical food laws. Before we do that, however, note that any health benefits we get from eating clean animals (or avoiding unclean ones) is not necessarily the reason God gave these commands. The text itself—in two consecutive verses—provides a different reason: holiness.

> For I am the LORD your God. Consecrate yourselves therefore, and be holy, for I am holy ... (Leviticus 11:44)

> For I am the LORD who brought you up from the land of Egypt to be your God; thus you shall be holy, for I am holy. (Leviticus 11:45)

Holiness means separation from the normal. God tells His people to avoid eating unclean animals to set apart His people. Several New Testament passages affirm the importance of holiness. In my favorite example, the Apostle Peter actually quotes Leviticus 11:

> As obedient children ... [be] like the Holy One who called you, be holy yourselves also *in all your behavior*; because it is written, "You shall be Holy, for I am Holy ..." (1 Peter 1:14–16, emphasis mine)

While the role of holiness in a believer's life is a whole other topic, we will do well to remember that it is common theme throughout the Bible—including Leviticus 11.

It is the only reason God gives for His dietary laws.

Eat Whatever You Desire?

As the Torah draws to a close, and the Israelites are about to enter the Promised Land, God tells the Israelites that they may eat whatever meat they want.

> When the LORD your God extends your border as He has promised you, and you say, "I will eat meat," because you desire to eat meat, then you may eat meat, *whatever you desire*. (Deuteronomy 12:20, NASB, emphasis mine)

Just as with Noah, though, "whatever" does not necessarily mean "all." The translators of the New International Version (NIV) seem to agree:

> When the LORD your God has enlarged your territory as he promised you, and you crave meat and say, "I would like some meat," then you may eat *as much of it as you want*. (Deuteronomy 12:20, NIV, emphasis mine)

Rather than negating God's clear instructions in Leviticus 11, this verse more likely casts a vision of abundance for what life will be like in the land flowing with milk and honey.

What God Says about Our Food, So Far

From the beginning, God has provided much guidance about what we eat. In Genesis 1:29, He gives Adam an abundance of plant-based foods on which to live. Later, God provides Noah with meat to eat; here the distinction between clean and unclean animals first appears. Later, in Leviticus 11 (and again in Deuteronomy 14), God more explicitly deems scavenger animals, like pigs, vultures and shellfish, off-limits for human consumption. While not all unclean animals are scavengers, it is useful to think in these terms as we continue to ponder God's perspective on food.

Questions to discuss and ponder

1. What appearances does food make in the Garden of Eden? How does this inform us about God's view of food? What are Genesis 1:29 foods? How do they fit into your diet?
2. Discuss the command given to Noah to take seven pairs of clean animals and only one pair of unclean ones (Genesis 7:2). Why do you think God gave that command to Noah? How do you think Noah knew the difference?

3. In Genesis 9:3 God opens the door to meat-eating. Why do you think He did this? Do you think He allowed all animals to be eaten or only certain ones? Why?
4. What is the Torah? Why was it given? Was it ever meant to justify people before God? To whom was it given?
5. What are the general guidelines for the food laws given in Leviticus 11? Do you think they still apply today? If not, why? If so, to whom do you think they apply? Why?

Endnotes

[1] Russell, Rex, MD *What the Bible Says about Healthy Living*. Regal, 1996. p. 105.

[2] Russell, p. 46

[3] See pages 99 to 104 in *The Maker's Diet* (Rubin) for a discussion about several myths about vegetarianism, including the theory that we can meet 100% of our nutritional needs without any animal products. This topic is also extensively addressed in *Nourishing Traditions* (Fallon).

[4] Technically, their time on the ark might have allowed unclean animals to reproduce. Because of the original numbers chosen, however, I still think that the plan was to avoid eating and sacrificing unclean animals.

[5] For example, see Genesis 13:5; 24:35; 26:14; 29:2–3, 8.

[6] Strong's H1241

[7] Strong's H6629

[8] Joshua 1:8

[9] For example, see Jeremiah 26:4–5.

[10] Psalm 19:7–11, Psalm 119

[11] Matthew 5:17–19

[12] 2 Timothy 3:16

[13] James 1:25

[14] Deuteronomy 22:11–12

[15] Leviticus 23

[16] Galatians 3:24

[17] For deeper study of Messiah in the Hebrew Scriptures, see *Messiah in the Old Testament* (Walter Kaiser), *Answering Jewish Objections to Jesus, Volumes One & Two* (Michael L. Brown), *What the Rabbis Know about the Messiah* (Rachmiel Frydland), or FFOZ's *Torah Club Volume Two*.

[18] 1 Samuel 13:14

[19] Deuteronomy 4:6–8

[20] Rubin, Jordan. *The Maker's Diet*. Siloam, 2004. p.34

[21] For more information about saints from the Hebrew Scriptures being credited with righteousness because of their faith, see Genesis 15:6, Habakkuk 2:4, Romans 4:22, Galatians 3:6, 21, James 2:23 and Hebrews 11.

[22] Exodus 14:31 makes it clear that the Exodus event included spiritual as well as physical redemption.

[23] For other examples of the Torah affirming its application to non-Hebrews, see Leviticus 16:29, Leviticus 18:26 and Numbers 9:14.

[24] God makes it clear that sacrifices are only permitted in the place that He chooses. (See, for example, Deuteronomy 12:5–13.) In 2 Chronicles 7:12, He names this place: the Jerusalem Temple.

[25] Instructions for the high priest: Leviticus 16; sacrifices to be made at the Jerusalem Temple: Deuteronomy 12:5–6; obeying the law of the land: Romans 13:1–7.

[26] To take it a step further, read the rest of Leviticus 19 and try to classify the commands into moral, civil and ceremonial. The distinctions are not as clear as you might think.

[27] Rabbits are also ruminants, but they do not qualify as food, since they do not have hooves, split or otherwise. (Leviticus 11:6) Four animals are listed in Leviticus 11:4–7 as having one sign, but not both. These four animals (the camel, the hyrax, the hare and the pig) are discussed in Rabbi Nosson Slifkin's book, *The Camel, the Hare & the Hyrax*. Here Slifkin speculates that these four animals were singled out by God as an extra precaution, since they were commonly eaten by the Israelites' Middle Eastern neighbors.

[28] See Matthew 3:4 and Mark 1:6.

[29] Genesis 1:21, 25

Did God Flip a Coin?
Scientific Support for the Biblical Food Laws

My life's biggest "Aha!" moments have come from realizing that the same God who created the universe also designed every aspect of human life. For example, my 15-year string of disastrous dating evaporated when I learned God's wisdom for biblical dating, marriage and sex.

Believe that marriage was designed to be based on mutual sacrifice and centered around God? Revolutionary! View physical intimacy as an expression of love flowing out of a lifelong commitment—rather than a prerequisite for it? Utterly liberating! God has a plan for my love life! I could finally check out of therapy and throw away the self-help books. The vision for Christian marriage was so compelling that I couldn't help but become a follower of Jesus.

But some "wisdom" about Christian sex and marriage—like people quoting Bible verses to prove that God forbids sex outside of marriage—was not helpful.

Only after a long process of studying, pondering and experiencing the blessings of God's wisdom for male/female relationships has my perspective on this topic shifted, not from someone pounding me over the head with Bible verses.

The same is true for my investigation of biblical eating. I "knew" that the Bible forbade consuming certain animals. Yet before I understood how God's designation of clean and unclean meat fit into His overall plan for mankind's diet, I struggled to let go of some of my most favorite foods.

For this reason, I do not want to pound you over the head with Bible verses. As we explore whether God cares about what we eat,

I want to be helpful. If you are like me, understanding the wisdom behind a Bible command can be as powerful as the command itself, so let's take a "time out" from our Bible study to see science's perspective on the biblical food laws.

Did God Flip a Coin?

God's design for marriage, for money stewardship, for servant leadership—it seems like God has wisdom for every subject imaginable. Following God's Word in these matters brings good results. This makes me wonder: why did God designate some animals as clean and others as unclean? Is pork's compatibility with the human digestive system really any different from cows'? Or did He just flip a coin to determine which would be which? Are the commands set forth in Leviticus 11 and Deuteronomy 14 arbitrary? Or is there some kind of hidden wisdom in the dietary laws that we have overlooked?

Many traditional interpretations—both Christian and Jewish—claim that there is no rhyme or reason for God's classification system. But this perspective implies that God essentially pulled names out of a hat when deciding how to categorize His many creatures. It also implies that our bodies, which He carefully designed, are totally indifferent to what we ingest.

I don't buy it.

Look at the intricate relationship between humans and plants—our prime food source per Genesis 1:29. One of our most basic needs is air to breathe (oxygen). The result of our breath—the associated waste that we exhale—is carbon dioxide. Plants, on the other hand, thrive on carbon dioxide, which we discard. Their output? Oxygen. Just as "One man's garbage is another man's gold," so too with the waste products of both plants and humans, which become vital sources of life for each other.[1]

Given the wisdom behind God's intelligently designed plant kingdom, it is not surprising that He also carefully crafted the animal kingdom. Let's see why it is highly unlikely that the clean/unclean designation is random.

Cows Versus Pigs

Think back to grade school science class: do you remember the difference between "omnivores" and "herbivores"?

Here is a hint: herbivores do not eat meat; they generally eat plant-based foods. Omnivores, on the other hand, eat everything—both plants and animals, including those animals that God calls unclean, like rats, spiders and cockroaches. Given their innate diets, would you rather eat an herbivore or an omnivore?

Interestingly, clean mammals—like cows—are inherently designed to be herbivores. God hard-wired them to eat plant-based foods—the same ones He gave to man in Genesis 1:29. Because they do not eat the flesh of other animals, they avoid many of the diseases, parasites and worms that other animals may carry. This makes herbivores healthier to eat than omnivores.[2]

The prevalence of Mad Cow Disease—caused in part by cattle being fed ground-up cattle brains and other remains—is an example of the consequences of circumventing God's plan for bovine vegetarianism. Dr. Don Colbert, a Christian physician, explains how this happens:

> As cattle [were] slaughtered, part of the remains of the cattle were used to make cattle feed. Cattle are herbivores, but slaughterhouses [added] leftover brains, bones, blood, and other cattle parts from slaughtered animals … to cattle feed … to enable them to grow larger and faster. In Britain, the remains of diseased cattle were mixed into the feed, allowing the disease to develop and spread rapidly.[3]

In August 1997 the U.S. banned feeding protein from cud-chewing animals (ground-up cows) to other cud-chewers. Unfortunately, not all cattle farmers follow this rule, which is difficult to enforce. This rule also does not prevent cattle from being fed ground-up animal parts from other, non-cud-chewing animals like cats and dogs.[4] In fact, according the United States Food and Drug Administration (FDA), processed chicken feathers, floor wastes from chicken coops and plastic pellets are all permitted in cattle feed.[5]

Remember that one of the characteristics of animals designated as clean in Leviticus 11 is that they must "chew the cud,"

Did God Flip a Coin?

which is a complex digestion process. Known as "ruminants," these animals essentially regurgitate their food for another pass at chewing. Yum. Once I can get beyond this aspect of God's design, I am fascinated. God gave ruminants a unique, multi-stomach digestive system that removes toxins from their food, before it is absorbed into their flesh. Dr. Colbert compares the ruminant's stomach to a washing machine that has four wash and rinse cycles. Like a washing machine running through its cycles, the ruminant's four stomach chambers must each digest the food before it is properly metabolized.[6] The food is expelled upward for re-chewing after it has entered the second pouch, but before it reaches the third. By the time their Genesis 1:29 food has reached their flesh, it is nearly free from anything that might be harmful to humans.

Another telltale sign of an herbivore is the length of its digestive tract. These vegetarian animals obviously need a lot of internal real estate to properly digest their food. As such, their digestive tracts are often six to twelve times the length of their bodies, which gives them time to completely process and eliminate any toxins or poisons.[7]

Herbivores' natural instincts would lead them to a diet of grains, grass and other vegetation.[8] As one of the clean animals listed in Leviticus 11, cows seem to be designed to be eaten by people, since their meat—in its God-given state—would be free from contaminants.

On the other hand, omnivores do not chew the cud and are designed quite differently. Pigs, for example, have a simpler, shorter digestive system that does not detoxify their food before it reaches their flesh.[9] Considering pigs as a food source is troublesome. Why? Because on their own, pigs will eat everything, including mice, dead animals and feces.

God designed these unclean animals intelligently—but as an environmental cleaner, not a food source. Scavengers were created with a purpose. They were created to clean up anything left dead in the fields, but they were not created to be eaten.[10] Dr. Rex Russell provides an interesting example of this intelligent design:

> Pigs have eaten Philadelphia's garbage and sewage for more than 100 years, saving the city $3 million a year in

landfill costs. This is a wise use of hogs. They are designed to clean our environment.[11]

Can present-day farmers and scientists breed and raise pigs that do not consume such foul food? Of course. But I am captivated by God's thoughtful, careful design for the animal kingdom, so erring on the side of caution, I avoid eating those intended to clean the environment, regardless of the "scientific advances" man has made. Besides:

> Even hog farmers who insist that corn-fed hogs are safe won't ... guarantee that their indoor hogs haven't eaten any rats, mice, fecal waste, or maggots within the past few days.[12]

Scientific studies support the apparent wisdom of the biblical food laws. A Johns Hopkins University study illustrates how pigs and other unclean mammals, birds, fish and insects have significantly higher toxicity levels than clean ones, like cows.[13] Another study, in which medical students were fed organic pork that was trichinosis-free, revealed serious changes in the subjects' blood chemistry after the pork was eaten.[14] The longer-term study could not be completed, since the subjects stopped eating pork after the initial testing.[15]

Fish

God's distinction between clean and unclean fish seems similarly planned. The two requirements for clean fish are fins and scales—characteristics notably absent in bottom-feeders that live where garbage, dead fish and excretions settle. I marvel at the clearly designed purpose for these scavengers. For example, shellfish can remove cholera from the sea. This toxic pollutant, which is associated with raw sewage, is miraculously absorbed by shellfish without making them sick. Effectively purifying the water, "clams and oysters can filter between twenty and fifty gallons of seawater a day."[16] In addition, raw shellfish, like oysters, are known carriers of viral hepatitis, which can lead to cirrhosis, liver failure and liver cancer.[17]

On the other hand, God clearly made clean fish to nourish humans. Species like salmon, mackerel, sardines and herring are especially rich in omega-3 fatty acids. These "essential fatty acids" have a variety of benefits, which include preventing heart attacks, lowering blood pressure, and easing arthritis, migraine headaches and asthma.[18]

Today, however, studies confirm that many fish—including those that God perfectly designed for human consumption—contain poisonous mercury. Should we be scared away from the seafood counter? My hope is that God's clear, biblical permission to eat fish with fins and scales, combined with His carefully crafted plan for our food, will somehow redeem fallen man's propensity to mess things up. Dr. Rex Russell provides evidence that might support this theory:

> Do you remember being frightened by the publicity about mercury being found in tuna fish? Actually, the alkylglycerols in the lipids of this clean fish pull out the toxic mercury from its flesh. When we eat the fish, the alkylglycerols also remove mercury and other heavy toxic metals from our bodies.[19]

How's that for God thinking ahead? If you believe that He can raise the dead to life, this should not be a stretch. While the jury is still out on this, I believe that for most folks, eating modest amounts of God-given, nutrient-rich fish fosters good health, in spite of the mercury risks.

The most important thing is not to become paralyzed. If we become obsessed with eating only perfectly healthy food, we will make ourselves—and those around us—crazy. In a world filled with Wi-Fi, microwaves, computers and cell phones, we only have so much control over our environment. We should do whatever we can to make good choices and to help change the world around us—without becoming burned out. Then pray for God to handle the outcome.

Birds

In Leviticus 11 God prescribes which birds to avoid eating, rather than listing those we may eat. Not surprisingly, most of these birds are scavengers, designed by God to help clean our environment. Included in their diets are carcasses, lizards, rats and other animals designated as unclean. Some will eat dead human flesh.[20]

By process of elimination, chicken, turkey, duck, goose and quail are considered clean by most authorities. Their digestive systems are quite different from those of scavenger birds. A chicken's primary diet consists of grasses and grain, and its craw (part of its digestive system) is similar to the cow's rumination pouches.[21]

Low in calories and fat, and high in cancer-fighting niacin, immune-boosting selenium, and metabolism-enhancing vitamin B6, chickens seem to be designed by God for us to eat. In fact, "The prostaglandins in chicken have strong antiviral properties. (Maybe your mother's chicken soup *is* good for the flu and colds.)"[22]

As with fish, God's original, intelligent design for clean birds has become somewhat obscured by man's intervention. Cramming chickens into close quarters and feeding them genetically modified grains and antibiotics reduces their health benefits to us. Thankfully, consumers are becoming more aware of these conditions, which are detrimental to both animals and humans, and some food producers are responding to the public's demand for free-range, chemical-free birds.

Insects

The New Testament is filled with indirect confirmations of the food laws in Leviticus. Jesus feeds thousands with presumably clean fish. He and the disciples celebrate the Passover feast, presumably by eating lamb, a clean meat. Jesus casts out a legion of demons from a man and into a herd of swine, who tumble off a cliff. Since He was an advocate of feeding the hungry, He probably did not consider the 2,000 hogs a valid food source.

We do, however, see one direct affirmation in Matthew 3:4 and Mark 1:6. John the Baptist is eating locusts, one of the few insects God designates as clean. While it might sound grotesque to us, there is scientific evidence that grasshoppers and locusts are healthy food choices. On a remote island off the coast of Korea, a small community eats a concoction that includes ground up locusts and grasshoppers. With little disease and record-breaking life-spans, they make a good case for the diet followed by John the Baptist.[23]

Perhaps designating locusts as clean is an example of God's grace. When God's judgment came upon the Israelites in the form of swarms of locusts that devastated their crops, they could at least sustain themselves by eating the little critters who caused the damage, thereby avoiding total famine.

Practically speaking, I am not eager to dine on chocolate-covered grasshoppers. But it is interesting.

How Are Humans Designed?

Are we designed to eat meat, or are our vegetarian friends correct in thinking that meat is to blame for humanity's ills and our shortened lifespan? Only God knows for sure, but physiologically we appear to be designed to eat meat—but not as the main part of our diets. Unlike herbivores such as cows, we have canine teeth—but not as many or as sharp as true carnivores, like wolves, who eat mostly meat. Unlike the herbivore's complex digestive system, ours is shorter and simpler—but not as short or simple as omnivores', like pigs. True meat-eaters' stomachs have far more hydrochloric acid than ours do, and their shorter digestive system enables them to digest and eliminate meat much faster than we can.[24]

Scripture shows that eating meat was often limited to special occasions: Kill the fatted calf! Slaughter the Passover lamb! Today, on the other hand, we probably eat too much meat. Farmers pump up their livestock with growth hormones and antibiotics, in part because we continue to increase our demand for meat. If we collectively reduced the quantity and frequency of our meat-eating, demand would ease, so supply would not need artificial stimulation. God probably designed us to eat clean poultry, fish and red meat like everything else—in moderation.

Isn't He Smart?

Have I fully proven that clean animals are healthy, and unclean animals are unhealthy? Probably not.[25] My goal is to simply present some information to chew on and pray about before we jump back to the Scriptures. Just as I was convinced of God's wisdom for marriage and sexuality when I understood its logic and benefits, I hope that seeing the practical side of the Bible's dietary standards encourages you to press on in the Scriptures.

I leave you with a few quotes from the experts:

> I am urging you ... to take another look at these laws, not for the spiritual purposes of salvation ... Rather, I am urging you to look at these laws *for the purpose of glorifying God through acknowledging His desire and design for health.*[26]

> There is no portion of the commandments of God in general, or of the Mosaic code in particular, that is not based on a scientific understanding of fundamental law. The laws of God are enforced and are as sure as the law of gravity.[27]

> The Israelites of antiquity followed a diet established by God and were consistently healthier than all of their neighbors. Regardless of your religious preference, any honest student of the Scriptures must admit that the wisdom of the Bible extends far beyond the spiritual issues to encompass every area of life—including dietary ... guidelines.[28]

Questions to discuss and ponder

1. Does the quoting of Bible verses help or hinder your learning process? Give examples. If it hinders your learning process, what learning methods do you find more helpful?
2. Describe how God designed cows and pigs and how their design might relate to our eating choices.
3. Describe how God designed different kinds of fish and how their design might relate to our eating choices.
4. Describe how God designed different kinds of birds and how their design might relate to our eating choices.
5. Describe how God designed different kinds of insects and how their design might relate to our eating choices.

Endnotes

[1] Russell, pp. 107–108

[2] Tessler, Gordon. *The Genesis Diet.* Be Well Publications, 1996. p. 50.

[3] Colbert, Don, MD *What Would Jesus Eat?* Thomas Nelson, Inc., 2002. p. 56.

[4] Lyman, Howard F., *Mad Cowboy: Plain Truth from the Cattle Rancher Who Won't Eat Meat.* Scribner, 2001. pp. 12–13.

[5] "You are what they eat," a report in the January 2005 issue of *Consumer Reports*, p. 26.

[6] Colbert, p. 13

[7] Tessler, p. 50

[8] Goats' reputation for eating tin cans and clothing is a myth. While their intense curiosity may lead them to nibble on non-plant food, they are indeed herbivores.

[9] Tessler, p. 51

[10] Josephson, Elmer A. *God's Key to Health and Happiness.* Revell, 1976. p. 47.

[11] Russell, p. 160

[12] Tessler, p. 52

[13] This study is cited by Russell, pp. 150–153.

[14] Fallon, Sally. *Nourishing Traditions: The Cookbook that Challenges Politically Correct Nutrition and the Diet Dictocrats.* New Trends Publishing, 2001. p. 32.

[15] Fallon, p. 76

[16] Colbert, pp. 38–39

[17] Russell, p. 47

[18] Colbert, p. 42

[19] Russell, p. 147

[20] Tessler, p. 58

[21] Russell, p. 148

[22] Russell, p. 147

[23] Russell, p. 64

[24] Colbert, p. 10

[25] There are some obvious exceptions to the clean/healthy and unclean/unhealthy generalizations I have made. For example, the unclean rabbit is considered to be a healthy source of protein. The clean carp is a bottom-feeder. *In general*, however, the health benefits of clean meats, and the toxicity of unclean ones, is difficult to refute.

[26] Russell, p. 26, emphasis his.

[27] Josephson, p. 160

[28] Rubin, p. 34.

What Would Jesus Eat?
First-Century Judaism's Historical Background

As disciples of the Master, we sometimes ask ourselves, "What Would Jesus Do?" The acronym WWJD appears on everything from bumper stickers to bracelets. Most Christians sincerely want to know what Jesus would do, because they truly want to follow His example.[1] After all, Jesus had a perfect track record of discerning and doing God's will.[2] This means that in any situation, determining what Jesus would have done provides us with insight into God's will. We want to imitate Jesus because He lived a life of perfect righteousness. His perfection—His sinlessness—qualified Him to be our atoning sacrifice,[3] but what did it mean for Jesus to be sinless? It meant that He did not deviate one iota from God's true, objective standard for living: His Bible, which included the Hebrew Scriptures' food guidelines.

Dr. Don Colbert points out that most Christians rarely ask the question, "What would Jesus eat?" Hence the title of his book, *What Would Jesus Eat?* It is a great question. What would Jesus eat? He would only eat the plant-based foods God provided in Genesis 1:29 and the animals designated clean in Leviticus 11.

Some folks believe that Jesus was eager to do away with the food laws, but the Torah itself says, "Whatever I command you, you shall be careful to do; you shall not add to nor take away from it." (Deuteronomy 12:32) Given Jesus' perfect obedience to God's Word, ignoring this verse and taking away the food laws would immediately make Him a sinner, ineligible to be our perfect sacrifice. Thankfully, Jesus Himself affirms that He did not come to do away with or in any way change the Torah.[4]

It is no surprise that Jesus obeyed God's Word and therefore ate only clean animals. What about His contemporaries? Were they secretly hankering for baby back ribs or shrimp scampi? Probably not.

To any Torah-observant person of Jesus' day, eating an animal that God designated as unclean would be abhorrent. Think about it. How do we react when another culture eats dogs, cats or horses—animals that we do not consider food? How much more repulsed would we be knowing that God's Word also forbids it? Even during the early first century, when several different sects of Judaism (such as the Pharisees, Sadducees, Essenes and the Way[5]) each interpreted the Scriptures differently, they all agreed that only those animals designated fit for human consumption per the Scriptures would be considered food.[6] Knowing that Jesus and His disciples most likely followed Leviticus 11's definition of food sheds some light on early first-century life.

The picture becomes even clearer when we examine the centuries immediately preceding Jesus. Just as it is important to watch the first act of a play to understand the second act, we need to understand the first century's historical background before we dive into the New Testament. Let's step back and review Israel's history:

- After the Exodus from Egypt, God gives the people of Israel (and the mixed multitude—that is, non-Jews—who accompanied them) the Torah at Mount Sinai.
- For the next thousand years the Israelites repeatedly fall into the following sin-cycle:[7]
    - They fall into idolatry, living like their pagan neighbors and worshipping their gods. In doing so, they drift away from God and living out His Word (Torah).
    - God lifts His veil of protection over them, so they suffer dire consequences at the hands of their enemies.
    - At the urging of a judge, prophet or wise king, they cry out to God and repent of ignoring Him.
    - God delivers them from their situation, using both human heroes and supernatural events.

- The people return to living out their faith through obedience to God and His Word (Torah).
- Because their obedience often yielded fruit, they again take Him for granted, believing that their blessed lives have come from their own efforts. They begin to drift away again ...

* The cycle of sin eventually "hits bottom," culminating in the Assyrian and Babylonian exiles in 721 and 587 BC, respectively. Many people are carted off to these foreign lands; others die from famine, plagues and slaughter. Things are really bad.
* The exiles' survivors return to Israel around 536 BC.

At this point, Israel's leadership sobers up. Perhaps we can imagine how the men in charge pondered how to prevent another such disaster: "In spite of God's love and faithfulness to us, we were disobedient to Him and His Torah. We fell into gross sin and idolatry, so we have suffered grave consequences. Let's think about how to keep from veering off course again."

This was a good idea. When God gave the Israelites the Torah a thousand or so years earlier, He warned them not to succumb to the pagan lifestyles of the Promised Land's original occupants. Examples of this detestable behavior included child sacrifice and witchcraft.[8] Unfortunately, the Israelites ignored God's instructions, commingled with the pagan population around them, and succumbed to their worldly ways of living.

Upon return from exile, Israel's Sages saw the error of their ways and hoped to reverse course. But with such a long, dismal track record, how could they turn around such a big ship?

Building a Fence

The "Great Assembly" was a group of Jewish leaders committed to preventing Israel from backsliding. Included in this group was the learned scribe Ezra, who "set his heart to study the law of the LORD and to practice it, and to teach His statutes and ordinances in Israel." (Ezra 7:10)

The Sages and elders of this era proposed to do this by commanding their disciples to "Be prudent in judgment, raise up many disciples, and make a fence around the Torah." (*Pirkei Avot* 1:1/ Ethics of the Fathers) Over 2,000 years later, this extra-biblical work of the Jewish Sages remains a cornerstone of Judaism.

Christians can certainly resonate with the call to good judgment and with making disciples. But what does it mean to "make a fence around the Torah"? Israel's leaders, in their desire to see their flocks thrive and hold fast to God and His teachings, began to erect "spiritual" protective barriers to keep out the influences that had repeatedly enticed the people into disobedience. The elders hoped that this would protect the masses from again falling away from God and His Word.

Our modern-day Christian shepherds sometimes establish similar fences to protect their people. For example, a church might discourage male pastors from counseling female congregants to prevent them from falling into sexual immorality or even presenting the appearance of it (1 Thessalonians 4:3). While Jesus did not necessarily follow this particular rule, common-sense, man-made guidelines like this often help folks avoid stumbling into sin.

Similarly, Israel's elders began to establish laws that would prevent the people from even getting close to violating God's biblical commands. These man-made laws, or traditions, became known as the "Oral Torah" (or "Oral Law") because they were passed down orally for hundreds of years before they were eventually codified in the *Mishnah*, less than two centuries after Jesus' death and resurrection.

Many of these man-made laws did, in fact, help restore Israel's focus on God and His Word. For example, the traditions that comprise the familiar Passover *seder*, which reminds God's people of their deliverance from Egypt, was practiced in Jesus' era and is still used today. Jesus Himself kept the *seder* traditions with His disciples.

However, some of the oral laws were unbiblically divisive, and some were used as loopholes to avoid responsibilities. Perhaps it is these types of laws Jesus refers to in Matthew 23:4 when He says that the leaders "tie up heavy burdens and lay them on men's shoulders."

To ensure that the people of God avoided the potential snares of their pagan neighbors' evil influences, some of these traditions created a division between Jews and non-Jews. These rules limited observant Jews from interacting with their non-Jewish neighbors. This greatly hindered Israel's ability to reflect God to other nations. Serving as a light to the surrounding nations was one of the main purposes of God's chosen people:

> The peoples ... will hear all these statutes [the Torah commands] and say, "Surely this great nation is a wise and understanding people." For what great nation is there that has a god so near to it as is the LORD our God whenever we call on Him? (Deuteronomy 4:6–7)

By building tall fences around themselves, Israel wisely sought to avoid its familiar sin-cycles. But in many ways, the Israelites went too far. Soon the man-made traditions took on—in their eyes—the same authority as the Bible itself. The Oral Torah became such a part of the Jewish community that the distinction between God's Word and man's word became blurred.[9]

To some extent, the Sages' three-point plan successfully protected Israel from lapsing into the gross, external idolatry that led to its exile. But the man-made separation between Jews and non-Jews departed from God's mandate in Deuteronomy 4 to be a light to the nations. Knowing about this separation, and the fences that created it, will help us better understand the New Testament verses we examine in the next chapter.

The Hebrew Scriptures' Final Scene

About 100 years after their return from exile—and just four centuries before Jesus—the prophet Malachi reveals final instructions before the curtain closes on the Hebrew Scriptures.

First, in Malachi 3:6–7 God emphasizes that He does not change. This reminder of God's faithfulness comforted the Israelites about future judgment. These verses also remind us of God's constancy and unchanging character. As the New Testament curtain opens, we must remember this fact—and that His unchanging character is inextricably linked to His Word. We must also remember that Jesus and His disciples believed this same thing: God and His Word do not change.[10]

In line with His consistent character, God rebukes His people for neglecting His Torah's commands and again calls them to return to Him (3:7). In Hebrew the word translated "return" is *shuv*, which implies a complete turn around—mind, body and soul. He wants their hearts, and He wants them to obey His Word. It is not an either/or proposition. This has been God's constant plea since He gave the Torah a millennium earlier.[11]

Second, in Malachi 4:5 God announces that Elijah would be the forerunner of the Messiah, a prophecy important to both Jews and Christians.[12] I am intrigued by how central this verse is to Christianity, yet I have never heard any teachings refer to the verse that immediately precedes it:

> Remember the Law [Torah] of Moses My servant, even the statutes and ordinances which I commanded him in Horeb [Sinai] for all Israel. (Malachi 4:4)

In the same breath that Malachi names Elijah as forerunner to the Messiah, Malachi urges his readers to observe the Mosaic Law. The people of Israel would cling to both of these verses as they anticipated the coming redemption. Jesus and the New Testament writers undoubtedly heeded Malachi 4:4 as much as they did 4:5.

Intermission

Fast-forward to less than two centuries before Messiah's coming. The Greeks conquered Israel and attempted to Hellenize the people by drawing them away from God and from obedience to His Word. While many succumbed, a faithful remnant of Israelites clung to the Torah in the midst of persecution. Filled with zeal and dedication to God, they held fast to the Scriptures and refused to partake in what had become the norm.[13]

This refusal to enter mainstream culture resulted in persecution. The Greeks forced Jews to sacrifice swine in God's Holy Temple and forbade them from circumcising their sons "so that they might forget the Torah and change all their observances."[14] Jews were forced by the government to eat unclean meats; anyone who refused was put to death. The story of Eleazar, for example, tells of a noble scribe and man of God who willingly died because he refused to eat pork. You can read his story in the appendix of this book.

During this fierce persecution, a faithful remnant waged war against the oppressive Greek overlords. This faithful group was lead by Judah Maccabee. Judah, his family and their compatriots risked torture and death rather than abandon God or forsake Scripture. In 165 BC Judah and his followers miraculously defeated the Greeks. The commemoration of their miraculous victory inspired the festival of Hanukkah.

I marvel at these stories of passionate, faithful Jews who were devoted to God's Word and were willing to risk their lives to defend it. The richness and depth of these events make me realize that the Hanukkah story is way more significant than I ever thought. (Growing up I thought that it was just a Christmas-wannabe.) In fact, Hanukkah's significance was likely well known by early first-century Jews, just 165 years after those passionate freedom fighters defended their right to observe God's instructions. Since Jesus Himself was at the Temple during Hanukkah (i.e., the Feast of the Dedication) in John 10:22, Messiah and His disciples were likely familiar with the story of Judah Maccabee—and stories like Eleazar's.

The Second Act

Jesus and His contemporaries avoided pork and shellfish not just because "it is written," but also because it was woven into the fabric of who they were: dedicated people of God who clung to Him and His Word out of love and reverence. They lived in the shadow of the Hanukkah revolt. Their ancestors had sacrificed their lives for the sake of God's commandments. Jesus and His disciples were ready to do no less.

As the curtain on the New Testament is ready to open, let's ask ourselves again, "What would Jesus eat?" From our study thus far, we know that neither Jesus nor His disciples would have eaten unclean meat.

Questions to discuss and ponder

1. Is the phrase "What Would Jesus Do?" helpful to you? Why or why not? If you find it helpful, describe the circumstances in which you might use it or have used it fruitfully. If you do not find it helpful, what methods do you use for discerning God's will?
2. Do you think Jesus ate unclean meat? What about His followers? Why or why not? Does this impact your decision on what to eat? If so, how?
3. Give a quick overview of Israel's historical "sin-cycle." How did the Sages address this recurring problem? Do you think it was successful? Why? How did this history (and the Sages' solution) influence the people of Israel during Jesus' day?
4. How might the last prophet from the Hebrew Scriptures (Malachi) have influenced Jewish people during Jesus' day?
5. How might the events that inspired the Hanukkah story have influenced Jewish people during Jesus' day?

Endnotes

[1] Colbert, p. ix
[2] John 8:29
[3] 2 Corinthians 5:21
[4] Matthew 5:17–19
[5] Acts 24:14
[6] Because there is no historical evidence that this topic was debated within Judaism, we can be confident that all of the Jewish sects had the same interpretation and application of the Leviticus 11 meat laws. On the other hand, topics like how to observe the Sabbath or the role of non-Jews in the community were hotly debated and therefore frequently written about.
[7] Reading the book of Judges will give you a good feel for this cycle.
[8] Deuteronomy 18:9–12
[9] In the rabbis' defense, they cite Deuteronomy 17:11 ("According to the terms of the law which they teach you, and according to the verdict which they tell you, you shall do; you shall not turn aside from the word which they declare to you, to the right or the left.") as support for their biblically-based responsibility to make and implement authoritative guidelines for applying God's instructions to daily living. Jesus Himself seems to affirm the rabbis authority in Matthew 23:3.
[10] Deuteronomy 4:2, Psalm 119:152, Isaiah 40:8
[11] Deuteronomy 6:5, 10:12–13, 11:1,13, 26:16

[12] In Jewish tradition there is a place set for Elijah at the Passover *seder* table with the hope that Elijah will appear and usher in the Messiah's coming. Christianity believes this prophecy is partially fulfilled, as Jesus says that "John himself is Elijah who was to come" (Matthew 11:14) when referring to John the Baptist.

[13] The books of Maccabees illustrate this passion. They are part of the Apocrypha, books excluded from Protestant and Jewish Bibles, but included in the Catholic Bible. Most Jewish and Evangelical scholars regard them as important historical works, even though they are not part of the official canon considered God-breathed.

[14] 1 Maccabees 1:49

The New Testament View

Reconciling Apparent Contradictions
with the Hebrew Scriptures

Christian theologians have written reams of articles, books, commentaries and Bible footnotes about why Leviticus 11 is not applicable to believers. Before we examine the food-specific verses that they cite, let's look at three general phrases that are often used to set aside the entire Torah (the Law): "Messiah fulfilled the Law," "We are no longer under Law, we are under grace," and "Messiah is the end of the Law."

Could the original meaning of these three verses be different than what most of Christianity has historically taught? Here are some alternative interpretations to ponder.

"Messiah fulfilled the Law" (Matthew 5:17)

Believers often use this phrase to explain why the Torah commands do not apply to them. In this phrase's context, however, Jesus seems to call us to heed both the Torah and the prophets (who regularly called God's people back to the Torah). Put on your first-century goggles and give it a read. What do you think?

> Do not think that I came to abolish the Law or the Prophets; I did not come to abolish but to fulfill. For truly I say to you, until heaven and earth pass away, not the smallest letter or stroke shall pass from the Law until all is accomplished. Whoever then annuls one of the least of these commandments, and teaches others to do the same, shall be called least in the kingdom of heaven; but whoever

keeps and teaches them, he shall be called great in the kingdom of heaven. (Matthew 5:17–19)

Some say that because Jesus "fulfilled" the Law, we do not have to keep it. But if this were true, why would He encourage His disciples to keep the commands—and teach others to observe them—in the very next verse? Besides, if He fulfilled the law of "thou shalt not murder," does it mean that we are now free to murder? This may seem like an extreme example, but I think you get my point. Even though Jesus "fulfilled" the Law, I do not feel free to ignore it.

Instead, since heaven and earth are still around, I think Jesus came to expound on the Law and "fill it fully" with its complete meaning.[1] Rather than giving me a reason for letting go of the Hebrew Scriptures, Jesus has made the Torah more interesting and inviting to me—just as He did for the fellows on the road to Emmaus.[2]

"We are not under law, but under grace" (Romans 6:15)

The Greek word *nomos* is almost always translated "law" in the New Testament, but its meanings can vary greatly. I try to examine the context of a passage before I decide how *nomos* is being used.

For example, the "law" can refer to the Law of Moses—the Torah. Paul uses *nomos* to refer to the Torah in Romans 7:12, "So then, the Law (*nomos*) is holy, and the commandment is holy and righteous and good." Compare this with Paul's other uses of *nomos*. In Romans 8:2 he uses *nomos* to contrast the "law" (*nomos*) of the Spirit of life in Messiah with the "law" (*nomos*) of sin and death. Is it possible that in Romans 6:15 *nomos* does not refer to the Torah? Let's take a look.

No Greek word for "legalism" existed during Paul's day.[3] This means that if Paul were looking to describe the heavy burdens some religious leaders lay on their followers (see Matthew 23:4), he would have needed to find a way to describe legalism using different words. Stern suggests that Paul does this by using the Greek term *upo nomon*, which is translated "under law" and that means:

> ... living under the oppression caused by being enslaved to the social system or the mindset that results when the Torah is perverted into legalism.[4]

In other words, perhaps Paul uses "under law" to refer to a form of legalism.

Here is another possibility. Romans five and six refer to the freedom we have from the penalty and condemnation of the Law of Moses that results from its violation.[5] Perhaps Paul was using "under law" in Romans 6:15 to refer to being under the Torah's condemnation—something that we are freed from when we are in Messiah.

Wouldn't new believers be confused if Paul were telling them, "Here's God's written Word for you to study and live by. Just remember: it doesn't apply to you"? Rather, maybe Paul was saying something like, "Now remember, don't get overwhelmed and think that you have to suddenly do everything that's in the Torah to be right with God. If you miss the mark, or if it takes you a long time to absorb what's in here, or if you stumble, remember that you have been declared righteous in God's eyes. Messiah paid the penalty for our sins."

These various possible interpretations of Romans 6:15—combined with Jesus' words in Matthew 5:17–19—make me doubt that Paul was referring to the Torah. Besides, given its significance to God's people, could Paul have been concluding that Torah is no longer applicable? I do not think so.

"Messiah is the end of the Law" (Romans 10:4)

The word translated "end" in Romans 10:4 is the Greek word *telos*. Strong's[6] confirms what we could probably deduce: *telos* means the goal, what is being aimed at. In other words, the Torah's end, or goal, was to point to the Anointed One (Messiah) who would redeem God's people. While the Torah clearly points to Messiah, it did not vanish when He appeared; rather, through faith in Him and the gift of God's Spirit, the Torah comes alive! Alternatively, if you really think that "end" means "termination," then perhaps Jesus is the "end" of the Torah's condemnation. See my comments on Romans 6:15.

Food-Specific Verses

I am not naïve enough to think that these alternate interpretations can change 2,000 years of church teaching. I simply want to share why I am uncomfortable pointing to verses like Matthew 5:17, Romans 6:15 or Romans 10:4 as biblical justification for eating an Easter ham.

Now, let's move beyond the general verses and investigate specific passages that may seem to give "thumbs up" to lobster tail. If you have not already, get out your Bible. Read each section on your own first, without looking at any footnotes or commentaries. Then prayerfully ponder what it meant for the original listeners, and think about what it means for us today. Then read my view, which may give you a different "lens" with which to approach the passage.

Man Alive! There's More!
D. Thomas Lancaster elaborates on each of the following passages beginning on page 103.

Mark 7:1–23: Followers of Tradition

The NASB translators have supplied us with a useful heading[7] for this passage: "Followers of Tradition." As I read this section, I see religious leaders butting heads with Jesus over *how* His disciples are eating: with unwashed hands. Notice that *what* they are eating is not discussed.

The ritual hand washing referred to is one of the "traditions of the elders" spoken of in Mark 7:3. Is Jesus alluding to Torah commands? Or is He referring to something else?

From a quick skim, we might think that Jesus is referring to Leviticus 11:33–36, which describes how the carcass of an unclean animal can transfer its uncleanness to pots and cisterns. On its face, both Mark 7 and Leviticus 11:33–36 relate to the issue of clean and unclean. But think about it. The Leviticus verses are part of the Torah—Jesus' only Holy Scripture, His Bible. Would He really be speaking so disparagingly about God's Word? I think He is talking about something else—one of the man-made traditions described in chapter three. Do you remember the fences that the

Jewish Sages built to protect the people from accidentally violating God's commands? These traditional hand-washing rules are an example of these fences.

Man's Word Versus God's Word

In the Mark seven passage, Jesus chastises the religious leaders for elevating these man-made traditions to the same level as God's commandments.

The following chart of the Mark seven verses further illustrates this point. The first column shows Jesus' support for the Hebrew Scriptures. The second column challenges the religious leaders' elevation of man-made traditions.[8]

Affirms Written Law	Challenges Elevating Traditions
—	... teaching as doctrines the precepts of men. (v. 7)
Neglecting the commandment of God,	you hold to the tradition of men. (v. 8)
You are experts at setting aside the commandment of God	in order to keep your tradition. (v. 9)
... thus invalidating the word of God	by your tradition which you have handed down ... (v. 13)

Here Jesus whole-heartedly affirms the eternal nature of His Bible (the Hebrew Scriptures) and cautions against creating traditions or interpretations that conflict with God's written Word—including the Leviticus 11 food laws. That said, would He go on to negate God's commands in the verses that follow? We would do well to remember that the Pharisees' issue was ritual hand washing—not God's meat laws.

If Jesus was not using the remainder of this passage (Mark 7:14–23) to nullify the Levitical meat laws, then what was He talking about? Jesus cleverly uses the moment to illustrate a bigger point: just as there are some external things that can make a person ritually unclean, there are some internal things (like evil thoughts, greed, malice and pride) that can make a person's heart "unclean."

Man Alive! There's More!
D. Thomas Lancaster further explains Mark 7. See pages 103–108.

Acts 10: Peter's Dream

Can one man's dream change our need to follow God's commands?

When I share my views about God's design for eating meat, one of the first questions I hear is, "What about Peter's dream?"

In Acts 10, Peter had a vision of a sheet coming down from heaven. Filled with both clean and unclean animals, a voice commands him to "get up, Peter, kill and eat!" Peter objects, declaring that he has never eaten anything unclean (10:14). Since this happened three times, and since the voice commands him, "What God has cleansed, no longer consider unholy," (Acts 10:15) many Christians assume that God has revoked the meat commands of Leviticus 11. Can this be?

In the Hebrew Scriptures, Jacob dreamed about a ladder reaching from earth to heaven. Joseph dreamed that his brothers' sheaves of wheat bowed down to his sheaf. My favorite Bible dream was in Gideon's story. A man dreamed that a loaf of barley tumbled into the camp and struck a tent so hard that it flipped the tent upside down and flattened it! Are these dreams about home improvement tools, agriculture anomalies or culinary blunders? I think not. Neither do I think that Peter's dream was about food.

The best interpretation of a perplexing Scripture passage lies in the text itself. What does the text say?

We first notice that Peter himself was "greatly perplexed" by the vision (10:17) and reflected on its meaning (10:19). If Peter did not know what this dream meant, then I need to proceed with caution when I attempt to interpret it.

Peter's dream is nestled into a pivotal section of Acts that clarifies God's intentions about Jews and non-Jews in fellowship together. Up to this point, some of the Oral Torah had evolved into a very real barrier between the Jews and their neighbors. This practice was so prevalent that this was the case even among believers in Messiah (Galatians 2:11–13). While the original intent was understandable (stay separate from pagans to prevent backsliding into idolatry), the separation caused tension in the believing community's infancy. Besides, it contradicted the Torah.[9]

Peter's dream is indeed a revelation from God—but it is not about food. Rather, Peter sets the record straight about Jews and non-Jews being on equal ground when he declares, "God has shown me that I should not call any *man* unholy or unclean ..." (Acts 10:28, emphasis mine) The dream also made him realize that God does not show partiality (10:34). Finally, when he was challenged about eating with non-Jews, Peter defended his actions by retelling his dream. He viewed his dream as support for his decision to fellowship with Cornelius, not as justification for eating frog legs (11:5–18).

Man Alive! There's More!
Read D. Thomas Lancaster's in-depth chapter on Peter's vision. See pages 109–113.

"Eat anything that is sold in the meat market ..." (1 Corinthians 10:25)

Is Paul finally addressing those pesky food laws in Leviticus? Nope. A quick scan of 1 Corinthians 8–10 reveals the topic at hand: meat sacrificed to idols. On one hand, both Exodus 34:12–15 and Acts 15:29 make it clear that God's people should avoid eating meat that idol worshippers have sacrificed to their gods (or worse, participating in those rituals). On the other hand, since idols mean nothing to believers, they need not over-investigate the source of their meat. (Meat from pagan animal sacrifices was often sold in the regular meat markets.) In other words, do not knowingly eat meat sacrificed to idols, but do not make yourself (or your butcher) crazy trying to find out if it has been.

Man Alive! There's More!
For more on 1 Corinthians 8–10, Galatians 2:10–15 and Romans 14, see pages 115–121.

"Everything created by God is good, and nothing is to be rejected if it is received with gratitude ..." (1 Timothy 4:4)

By now I hope that when you read verses like this, you pause and ask yourself, "What does Paul mean? He's not talking about God's Word and Leviticus 11, is he? What issue could he be addressing?" The context of the passage usually answers these questions. In this case, the chapter's opening verses point to "doctrines of demons" and "deceitful spirits" for why some had fallen away from the faith. I simply cannot believe Paul, who observed the Torah,[10] would ever call the Torah—God's Word—"doctrines of demons." Paul's declaration that "everything created by God is good" is in response to man-made laws created by early Gnostics who taught abstinence from certain foods. This passage addresses these regulations—not those found in Paul's Bible in Leviticus 11.

Man Alive! There's More!
For more on 1 Timothy 4, Colossians 2 and other passages related to Gnosticism, see pages 123–127.

The Future is Invading the Present

Some Christians believe that Leviticus 11 and other Torah laws will again apply in the future. Dispensational theology holds that there is a "parentheses" during the Church Age in which believers are not bound by the Hebrew Scriptures' laws, which will become applicable again in the future. This idea of a Torah time-out seems odd.[11] If the Torah laws were applicable in the past, and they will be again in the future, I suggest that God still cares about them today.

Several years ago, I attended a conference where the speakers periodically looked forward to end times and declared "the future is invading the present." In other words, they saw modern-day glimpses of end-times prophecies in which the Torah is proclaimed and lived out.[12] I do not know the details of how God's story will unfold, but I resonate with their assessment that the Torah is becoming more and more revered by God's people.

The prophet Isaiah, in a passage that I believe still awaits fulfillment, hints about the future applicability of the Leviticus 11 food laws to God's people:

> For the LORD will execute judgment by fire and by His sword on all flesh, and those slain by the LORD will be many. "Those who ... eat swine's flesh, detestable things and mice, will come to an end altogether," declares the LORD. (Isaiah 66:16–17)

What does the New Testament say about this topic? While it does not mention meat specifically, John's Revelation points to a time when believers will esteem and live out God's Torah:

> So the dragon was enraged with the woman, and went off to make war with the rest of her children, *who keep the commandments of God and hold to the testimony of Jesus.* (Revelation 12:17, emphasis mine)

I believe that "the commandments of God" refers to His written Word—all of it, including Leviticus 11. And since "nothing unclean" will be brought into the New Jerusalem[13] where believers will experience eternal communion with God, perhaps we should start getting used to turkey bacon while we are still alive. You may disagree. But just remember that 2,000 years ago the most learned Bible scholars (Jewish) thought they knew what the future held regarding the Messiah's first coming. I believe they missed the mark. Today, many learned Bible scholars (Christian) think they know what the future holds about His second coming. I believe that many will miss the mark.

Living by the Book

It is clear to me that I don't have to follow the Hebrew Scriptures' laws as a means to gain right-standing before God. However, as part of my response to His loving presence in my life, and my desire to follow Him with my heart, mind, body and soul, I am excited to search His Word—all 66 books—to discover how He wants me to live.

Some Christian scholars affirm the importance of living by the whole book—including the Hebrew Scriptures. As I noted in chapter one, however, the Torah's laws are often classified as moral, civil and ceremonial, and only the moral ones are considered still applicable. Since the food laws in Leviticus are usually classified as ceremonial, these laws are presumed to be void.

I certainly see the logic behind this division. After all, some commands—like Temple sacrifices or those given to the priests—are not applicable without a Temple. It also means that others—like immersing in water and waiting until evening—are not necessary, since we will not be entering the Temple precinct anytime soon.

But isn't it possible that Christian scholars or the Early Church Fathers have misclassified verses here and there? What if our teachers' best attempts at discernment have missed the mark, and some of God's important commands have slipped through the cracks?

Seeing alternative ways to interpret familiar New Testament passages has helped me start to reconcile the Laws in the Hebrew Scriptures with the New Testament. I am finally convinced—in my head and my heart—that God and His Word do not change. As a result, I have come to believe that more of God's Word applies to me than I ever imagined. Rather than being a "burden," however, following more of His divine instructions has deepened my relationship with Him and revitalized my faith.

Questions to discuss and ponder

1. Do you think believers in Jesus should obey the laws in the Hebrew Scriptures? Why or why not? Is this a researched position or an inherited one? Describe. If you think the laws are applicable, which ones? Why?
2. Read and discuss Matthew 5:17–19. What do you think it means for Jesus to "fulfill" the law? How does this passage impact your view of the Torah?
3. Read and discuss Mark 7:1–23. What do you think is the religious leaders' issue with Jesus? What do you think is Jesus' issue with the leaders? Can you think of any similar issues that exist in the church today?
4. Read and discuss Acts 10. What do you think Peter's dream means? Why?
5. Do you think the Leviticus 11 meat laws will apply in the future? Why or why not?

Endnotes

[1] The word "fulfill" comes from a Greek word that can mean "fill up" or "make full." See Strong's G4137.

[2] Luke 24:13–31

[3] C.E.B. Cranfield, *The International Critical Commentary, Romans*, 1979, p. 853 as quoted in David Stern's *Jewish New Testament Commentary*, Jewish New Testament Publications, 1996, p. 536.

[4] Stern, p. 537 in his comments on Galatians 2:16b.

[5] Romans 5:9

[6] Strong's G5056

[7] Remember, Bible section headings are not in the original text; modern-day translators have created them, based on their understanding of the section.

[8] Jesus was mainly concerned with the traditions that contradicted the spirit and letter of the Torah.

[9] Recall from chapter one that according to the Torah, the community of God's people included both Jews and non-Jews (Numbers 15:14–16). Also, the whole purpose of God choosing the Israelites was to attract people from the surrounding nations to Him (Deuteronomy 4:6–8); this would be hard to do if there were no interaction!

[10] Acts 25:8

[11] For information about the flaws in dispensational theology, see Mathison, *Dispensationalism: Rightly Dividing the People of God?* Presbyterian and Reformed Publishing Company, 1995.

[12] Isaiah 2:3, Micah 4:2

[13] Revelation 21:27

Avoiding Blood, Fat and Things Strangled

Is *Kosher* Meat the Answer?

Since Noah's time God has prohibited eating blood.[1] God calls blood-avoidance "a perpetual statute throughout your generations." (Leviticus 3:17) Applicable to both Jews and non-Jews,[2] this command was affirmed by the prophets, who likened eating blood to idolatry.[3] King Saul chastised his subjects for eating meat with blood in it.[4] God equates eating blood-filled meat with the occult.[5] Even the New Testament affirms this command; in Acts 15 the Jerusalem Council agreed that new believers should avoid eating blood, which was a common pagan practice.

If we abstain from eating blood, the Bible promises that things will go well with us and our families.[6] Conversely, severe consequences may arise if we do eat blood: anyone who eats blood will be cut off from his people.[7]

The Big Deal about Blood *

Mentioned over 400 times, blood is one of the Bible's most often-repeated topics. It is clearly important to God. From Genesis to Revelation, blood is a common denominator. What's the big deal?

In the Bible, blood is regarded as more than part of a living organism's anatomy. Blood is a creature's life-force. The Bible says that blood contains the very soul. Eating blood is explicitly forbidden because "the life [literally the "life-force" or "soul"] of the flesh is in the blood." (Leviticus 17:11) Blood, its motion and flow, is the difference between a living body and a dead body. So long as blood is coursing through a creature's veins, it is alive. Hence, the soul is in the blood.

Beginning with the blood of Abel's sacrifices, to the blood of Abel himself, to the blood of circumcision, to the blood of the Passover lamb, to the blood of the Covenant, to the blood of the Temple sacrifices, to the blood of the Day of Atonement, to the blood of Messiah, to the souls of the righteous that have been "washed in the blood"—we revere a bloody book. When we understand the significance of the blood/soul relationship, we can understand what the big deal is.

In addition, understanding a little bit about blood's sanctity and its relationship to the soul helps us better understand the significance of Jesus' blood. When we speak of Jesus' blood, we are speaking of His life-force. To say that we are "washed in Jesus' blood" is to say that we are cleansed by His life—a resurrected and imperishable life. The blood He shed on our behalf was His very life-force.

Understanding this biblical perspective on blood also helps us better understand why we are urged to abstain from ingesting it.

* Many thanks to D. Thomas Lancaster for writing *The Big Deal about Blood*

Blood and Science

Why do morticians drain blood from corpses? To prevent decay. Similarly, "blood not drained out of an animal will flood that carcass with deadly putrefaction and disease."[8] Science agrees that abstaining from blood is a good thing, since it circulates throughout the entire body, transporting toxins and disease wherever it goes.

> Scientists have long known that blood carries infections and toxins that circulate in an animal's body. If people eat animal blood, they are needlessly exposed to these infections and toxins...Blood is the body's transport system, carrying in it all waste products for disposal.[9]

As with the unclean animals, maybe the purpose behind God's blood-avoidance commands is, in part, to care for His people's health.

How Do We Avoid Eating Blood?

Based on the biblical and scientific evidence, we would do well to avoid eating blood. How do we do this? A good start is not eating steak tartare (raw meat), blood pudding or blood sausage (yes, the last two are indeed made from animal blood). The next step is to always grill or broil meat until it is no longer pink inside. This removes the blood. With chicken, cooking it until the "juices run clear" is a common cooking instruction. If poultry's juices are clear rather than pink, much of the blood has likely been cooked out.

Another way to avoid eating blood is to avoid eating those scavenger animals that God calls unclean. For example, we indirectly eat blood if we eat pigs, vultures or other animals that eat other animals. Vegetarian animals like cows, however, do not ingest blood. Eating them, therefore, poses no risk of our eating blood so long as they have indeed eaten a vegetarian diet. Finally, eating kosher meat, or meat slaughtered in a kosher manner, is probably the best way for meat eaters to avoid consuming blood.

What Is *Kosher*?

The Hebrew word *kosher* literally means "straight" or "right" or "proper."[10] It is only used a few times in the Hebrew Scriptures,[11] but never in describing food. Over the centuries, however, *kosher* has evolved into a blanket term describing food that observant Jews eat. Today an entire sub-set of the food industry is devoted to the manufacture and oversight of *kosher* food.

Here are three main aspects of *kosher* food, as typically practiced by modern-day Orthodox Jews:

1. Animals labeled "clean" in Leviticus 11 are *kosher* for eating, but only if certain other standards are met (see my next two points). Those labeled "unclean" by God's Word, and foods made with associated by-products, can never be *kosher*. For example, pork bacon, ham or ribs are never *kosher*. Neither is chicken sausage that is stuffed into pork casing. (Sausage casing is made from animal intestines.) If the label says "natural casing," it is probably pork.

Lard, which is made from hog fat, would also be considered off limits. Other examples literally strain gnats.[12] "Resinous glaze" or "shellac" is made from ground up bugs and used to coat candy. "Carmine" or "cohineal" is a red food coloring made from dried bugs that is used in candy, fruit drinks and baked goods. "Civet" is used to flavor ice cream, candy and gum. It is made from civet cats. Label readers who usually breathe a sigh of relief when they see "natural flavorings" take heed: bugs and cats are considered "natural." Since these additives do not pass the Leviticus 11 test, foods that contain them are not considered *kosher*.[13]

2. *Kosher* meat is killed via special slaughtering technique, has had its blood completely drained, and has had certain fats and other body parts removed from it. I will discuss these aspects of *kosher* in this chapter. Today's *kosher* meat requirements exceed both biblical and governmental requirements.

3. *Kosher* eating mandates the separation of meat and dairy; I address this in the next chapter.

Some Christians think that *kosher* simply means that the food was blessed by a rabbi. Ironically, when I Googled "bless the food," I found only Christian websites and nothing about *kosher*. While blessings sometimes do take place, this is not the main point of certified *kosher* food. Rather, the *kosher* industry originally rose from the desire to submit to God's will, as the Sages discerned from Scripture and from other ancient wisdom.[14]

While it is uncertain how close modern *kosher* actual practices are to God's original intention, I do respect the biblical origins of these practices. Dr. Temple Grandin, a world-renowned professor of animal science at Colorado State University, affirms that the *kosher* method of animal slaughter was "state of the art humane" at its inception, and that its inspection process created the "original meat inspector."[15]

Kosher Meat: Steering Clear of Fat

Before we return to the issue of blood, let's focus on fat. Did you know that the Bible prohibits eating certain fats? In recent years, some folks have proclaimed the end of the "low-fat/no-fat" era. But perhaps there is biblical wisdom to avoiding certain animal fats.

Leviticus 7:23 explains that certain animal fats from oxen, sheep or goats are forbidden to be eaten. Verse 25 explains that these portions were to be set aside for the Lord. In Tabernacle/Temple times, this fat was to be part of the worshiper's sacrifice. Therefore, eating fat that surrounds certain organs, such as the kidneys and liver, is prohibited.[16] Throughout Leviticus, it is clear that the fat belongs to the Lord.

Does this apply to us? Even though we no longer offer sacrifices, I cannot help but wonder if our wise and loving Creator specifically chose for Himself those animal parts that are most harmful to humans—the animal's external suet, or covering fat, which is a suspected artery clogger and which stores up DDT and other deadly toxins. Not surprisingly, the observant Jewish community still follows this practice, even though the animals are not destined for the altar. The cover fat from these organs is never part of *kosher* meat.

Practically speaking, few of us eat organ meat. But what about ground beef used in hamburgers, meatloaf and spaghetti sauce? According to USDA regulations, ground beef may be up to 30% fat, so if your next trip to your favorite restaurant includes eating a hamburger, it probably includes some of the prohibited fat portions belonging to the Lord.

A few final points about fat. First, the Bible does not prohibit eating the fat contained within the animal's muscle. This makes sense. If the Bible deemed all animal fats off-limits, it would effectively eliminate eating any meat, eggs or dairy. Why would God promise a land "flowing with milk and honey" to the Israelites if they could not drink the milk? Why would God point out which animals may be eaten, if He did not allow us to eat them?

Second, both science and Scripture reveal that plant-based fats are actually good for us. For example, throughout the Bible, olives and olive oil are associated with health, anointing and abundance. Not surprisingly, science repeatedly affirms the health benefits of most Genesis 1:29-based fats such as olives, olive oil, avocados and walnuts.[17]

Kosher Meat: Biblical Slaughter and Preparation

The *kosher* method of slaughter (known as *shechitah* in Hebrew) can be traced all the way back to the slaughter of Temple sacrifices and to Moses and Aaron, who ensured that the animal offerings were properly bled.

Throughout the Torah, "slaughter" describes the process used to kill an animal for sacrifice to the Lord. Since these offerings were often eaten by priests, Levites and/or the offerers themselves, observant Jews see slaughter as the natural, biblical manner for killing an animal that will be eaten.[18] Perhaps this has application for believers, too. If our bodies are now God's Temple, maybe the method used to prepare meat for God's Temple thousands of years ago still has relevance for us today.

The Torah itself implies that some type of slaughter is needed to drain the blood from the animal before it is eaten. How else could blood be "poured" out?

> You may slaughter and eat meat within any of your gates … you shall not eat the blood; you are to pour it out on the ground like water. (Deuteronomy 12:15–16)

What Does *Kosher* Slaughter Entail?

Ideally, the highly trained *shochet* (ritual slaughterer) quickly cuts the animal's throat using a long, flawless, surgically-sharp knife. The jugular, trachea and esophagus must all be immediately severed in order for it to be *kosher*. The slightest pause during this process, the slightest nick in the knife, or the slightest rip or tear in the animal's flesh (rather than clean cut), renders the process invalid and the animal non-*kosher*. The cow's spinal cord must remain intact in order to keep the brain alive; this keeps the heart beating, pumping the blood out of the body. When done correctly, this quick loss of blood renders the cow unconscious.

To meet *kosher*'s strict standards, most *shochets* attend a special school for several years, work as an apprentice for a certified *shochet*, and pass rigid tests. The candidate's character and dedication to God must also be affirmed.

This intricate slaughter is just the first step in the meat *koshering* process. Once blood has been pumped out and the carcass has been rinsed off:

- Large veins that might still contain blood are removed.
- Fat surrounding certain organs (designated as the Lord's portion) are removed.
- The sciatic nerve is removed, according to the ancient tradition derived from Genesis 32:32.[19]

The next step is salting and soaking. To ensure that as much blood as possible has been drained, the meat is washed, salted (to draw out the blood), then repeatedly washed again to remove all traces of salt.[20] While this step is not part of the biblical mandate, Dr. Temple Grandin suggests that there may be a health benefit from it: it kills germs.

This process of slaughtering, removing select body parts, and salting/soaking enables *kosher*-meat eaters to dine virtually guaranteed of avoiding blood and biblically prohibited fat. But did Jesus only eat meat that was properly slaughtered and de-veined and rinsed and salted and rinsed again? Since He was sinless, He must have abstained from eating blood and certain fats. But how did He do it?

Many present-day *kosher* slaughter practices are, in fact, part of the *Mishnah*,[21] a compendium of ancient oral laws that were written down in the second century. Because many of these oral laws were part of the culture in which He lived, it is possible that Jesus only ate meat killed and prepared in this way. While *kosher* slaughter methods are technically a tradition, I believe that those methods—when properly carried out—are a great way to follow the Torah's commands to avoid eating blood and forbidden fats.

Kosher Meat: Benefits above and beyond the Call

I originally assumed that *kosher* meat was a well-intentioned tradition gone awry. It seemed to be an overly complex solution to the Bible's prohibition against eating blood and certain fats. The more

I learned about the detailed process that is used today, however, the more I discovered its wisdom and potential health benefits.

For example, in order to qualify as *kosher*, a cow's organs must pass rigorous tests. If it has perforated, missing or torn organs, or any fractured bones, the cow cannot be *kosher*. To test a cow's lungs, for example, a *bodek* (trained inspector) sticks his hand inside the cow's lungs to ensure that there are no adhesions or other deformities; these indicate that the animal might have had pneumonia or other sicknesses. If any of these occur, no part of the cow is *kosher*. However, animals that are rejected for *kosher* meat generally pass USDA standards, so they are often sold in the non-*kosher* market. Sick cows rejected by *kosher* inspectors are probably not healthy to eat, but selling them on the regular market is perfectly legal.

Who ensures that *kosher* meat packers weed out the cows that do not meet these high standards? A variety of certification agencies verify that all of the proper steps have been taken during the *kosher*ing process. These independent organizations impose strict consequences on companies that do not meet *kosher* standards, including loss of their certification. This is in addition to the scrutiny of the *shochet* himself, who is trained to inspect the animal.

What about Organic Meat?

As intriguing as the *kosher* process is, however, it only governs the end of an animal's life. How these animals are raised prior to slaughter is a whole other issue—and one that is not considered for the *kosher* meat designation.

An overview of the beef industry's two main players is important to better understand the story behind tonight's T-bone:

1. PRODUCERS/FARMERS: They raise the cattle and supply the meat. They choose their cattle's environment: will they graze on grassy fields, or will they be cooped up in cramped quarters and shackled? Producers decide what the cows eat. Grass? Grains? Animal by-products derived from euthanized pets and roadkill?[22] They also decide whether cows will be pumped up with steroids (for beefier cattle) and/

or antibiotics (to prevent the inevitable sickness that follows such unnatural treatment).

On one end of the spectrum, certified organic beef comes from well-coddled cattle that are raised under very specific conditions. Their mothers must be raised organically during the last trimester before birth. They are fed only organic food during their lifetime. They can never be injected with hormones or antibiotics. And if they are also grass fed, these cows live on open pastures as God designed, eating the food that God designed for them.

On the other end of the spectrum, cattle may be crammed together in institutional feedlots, dehorned, castrated, dipped in insecticide, injected with artificial hormones and fed processed sewage and poultry litter.[23]

Can you guess which type of cow is healthier for humans to eat? If it sounds like I'm painting a polarized picture of meat producers, I am. From what I can tell, today's cattle are either raised by companies that actively, intentionally care for the cows (often smaller, family farmers), or by giant "factory farms" that continually "improve" on God's design by using antibiotics, hormones and chemicals that beef up the bottom line at the animals' and the consumers' expense.[24]

2. MEAT PACKERS/DISTRIBUTORS: They buy their cows from producers. Meat packers kill the cows and process the meat, which is then shipped to your local grocery store or butcher. This step determines whether or not meat will be certified *kosher*, since some plants have the necessary equipment and people, and some do not. Note that the choice of meat supplier does not impact a cow's *kosher* eligibility, so it is possible for certified *kosher* meat to have been raised on antibiotics and growth hormones.

Perhaps grass-fed cows raised in a certified organic manner reflect God's design for how cows are supposed to live.[25] Perhaps cows killed in a certified *kosher* manner reflect His design for how

Avoiding Blood, Fat and Things Strangled   69

they are supposed to be killed for food. But the majority of meat consumed in the U.S. is subject to neither the organic nor the *kosher* certification oversight agencies. Who, then, regulates the meat sold in most grocery stores and restaurants?

The United States Department of Agriculture (USDA) is the oversight board for all meat sold in the U.S. In fact, meat processing may not take place in either *kosher* or non-*kosher* plants unless a USDA inspector is present. Unfortunately, the original benevolent intent behind this oversight has strayed quite far from its current reality. As such, the additional oversight provided by independent agencies (like organic and *kosher*) may well result in a higher quality of meat than USDA oversight alone provides.

Allowable Slaughter Methods

One of the areas that the USDA oversees is allowable slaughter methods. They require that only humane methods be used to kill livestock.[26]

For non-*kosher* meat packers, animals must be rendered "insensible to pain" before being cut, shackled or hoisted. Methods to accomplish this include:

1. A single captive bolt stun (essentially a gunshot), which is driven into the cow's brain.
2. Electric stunning applied to the head.
3. Stunning via carbon dioxide poisoning.

While *kosher* meat companies are subject to the USDA's authority, they are exempt from this particular rule, since the *kosher* method of slaughter, when done properly, causes the animal to instantly lose consciousness. Therefore, it is recognized as an equally humane way of slaughter. Some independent sources affirm the humane treatment of animals during the *kosher* slaughter process:

> If the slaughter is done in accordance with Jewish law and with the highest standards of modern animal handling practices, the animal will die without showing any signs of stress.[27]

Humane Treatment

Even if you are not an animal rights activist, the humane treatment of animals might concern you.

> Fear and pain in animals still alive produce hormones that can damage the meat. Also, fear in the animal still alive causes the muscles of the animal to contract and arteries to be constricted—this enables the animal to hold blood in its tissues and meat.[28]

It is not clear whether these fear hormones find their way into the humans who consume these animals. However, the blood retained in the animal's meat is problematic in light of Scripture's prohibition on eating blood.

In addition, several of God's commands reflect concern for animals. For example, cattle are permitted a Sabbath rest (Exodus 20:10). The Israelites were commanded to help a fallen ox or donkey (Deuteronomy 22:4) and to relieve an overburdened animal of its load (Exodus 23:5). A mother bird is to be driven away before her young are taken (Deuteronomy 22:6–7). As such, *kosher* slaughter was originally designed to be as humane as possible.

When describing the other USDA-approved methods of slaughter, some *kosher* advocates point out that we no longer execute humans via firing squad or electrocution, since they have been deemed inhumane, so why would we still use them on animals? The bolt gun "stun" method has a high failure rate—which means that animals may wake up before they are slaughtered. Workers with dull knives and production quotas must then contend with partially-conscious, twisting, squirming cows.[29]

At the same time, however, evidence against *kosher* slaughter is compelling. According to Temple Grandin, most of the major *kosher* slaughter plants often do not achieve the ideal slaughter outlined in this chapter.[30]

The truth about the humanity of *kosher* slaughter probably lies somewhere in between. Objective, scientific studies have shown that when properly slaughtered using *shechitah*, calm calves usually collapse immediately, and calm cattle collapse within 10 to 15 seconds.[31] However, it is difficult to know which *kosher* processors use humane (calm-producing) restraining devices and truly follow *shechita*'s high standards.

Biblical Ramifications

Scripture tells us to avoid eating blood. A variety of verses imply that "slaughter" is the way to accomplish this, simply by process of elimination. For example, animals that are "torn by beasts" or that die a natural death are not to be eaten (Leviticus 22:8). Strangled animals should also be avoided (Acts 15:29). While non-*kosher* cattle are eventually slaughtered, they sometimes die from the modern-day equivalent of strangulation. The common bolt stun method, for example, immediately destroys the brain. This causes the lungs to stop functioning, which deprives the animal of oxygen. This causes the animal to suffocate long before a knife is taken to its throat.

In other words, since the Bible uses the term "slaughter" when referring to meat that will be sacrificed and/or eaten, and the Bible mentions several other methods that are unacceptable, perhaps the *kosher* method of slaughter most closely matches God's intent of how animals are to be killed.

Conclusion

Rabbinic sources indicate that the details of the *shechitah* slaughtering process date back to well before Jesus' day. It is unlikely that Jesus Himself ever ate meat that was not slaughtered by the standards of *shechitah*. The Acts 15 prohibitions on blood and strangled meat also point in that direction. If blood and fat and things strangled were not part of Jesus' diet, and they will not be part of our diet when He returns,[32] then we ought to seriously question whether we should be eating them now. How we accomplish this on a practical, day-to-day basis, however, is an entirely different matter and subject to interpretation. Of course, we have to come to our own conclusions on these matters.

Ideally, the meat I buy for my family would be grass fed, certified organic and certified *kosher*. In America, organic meat and *kosher* meat are slowly becoming more available, but we usually must choose between the two.[33] In addition, the higher prices these meats command can be prohibitive.

When it comes to keeping "biblically *kosher*," there is obviously a continuum. At a minimum, we might consider abstaining from meats the Bible forbids as unclean. In a perfect world, the meat would also be certified organic, certified *kosher* and certified delicious. It is that perfect world that we are anticipating when Messiah comes. In that day, the Law will go forth from Zion[34] and every hamburger will be derived from a healthy, clean animal that was humanely raised, organically fed and biblically slaughtered according to the Torah's highest standard. In that day, I'll be loving it.

Questions to discuss and ponder

1. What does God say about eating blood or fat? How does this currently impact your food choices? How might your food choices change after further study?
2. Why is blood so important to God?
3. What are some practical ways to avoid eating blood or fat?
4. What is *kosher* food by today's Orthodox Jewish standards? What might a definition of "biblically *kosher*" be?
5. Describe the origins and current-day method of *shechitah* (the *kosher* method of slaughter). What are the advantages of eating certified *kosher* meat? What is certified organic meat? What are its benefits?

Endnotes

[1] Genesis 9:4
[2] Leviticus 17:10,12
[3] Ezekiel 33:25
[4] 1 Samuel 14:33–34
[5] Leviticus 19:26
[6] Deuteronomy 12:23–25
[7] Leviticus 7:26–27
[8] Tessler, p. 65
[9] Russell, pp. 28, 67
[10] Strong's H3787
[11] Esther 8:5, Ecclesiastes 10:10, 11:6
[12] Examples that follow are taken from Eidlitz, *Is it Kosher?* pp. 128–140.

[13] Certified *kosher* foods generally avoid these yummy additives. However, *kosher* certification does not guarantee that a product or its other ingredients are healthy for you.

[14] For excellent examples of the biblical basis for many kosher laws, see Aaron Eby's book *Biblically Kosher: A Messianic Jewish Perspective* (FFOZ, 2011).

[15] Personal communication with Temple Grandin. For more information about Dr. Grandin, or to read the dozens of articles and papers she has written on the topic of animal slaughter and restraining devices, visit her website at www.Grandin.com.

[16] Leviticus 3:9–10

[17] See Russell, pp. 125–142 for more information about God's design for eating fat.

[18] Interestingly, current-day *kosher* meat preparation practices are also retained, in part, for future reasons. When the Temple was destroyed in 70 AD, the Sages realized that Judaism was at risk of losing the slaughter methods that had been honed for over a thousand years. Therefore, to prepare for when the Temple is rebuilt (and sacrifices are reinstated), they still use ancient, traditional slaughtering methods. In other words, just as Jesus warned His followers in Matthew 25:13 to "be on the alert ... for you do not know the day nor the hour," observant Jews are always on the lookout for the Messiah's coming and His future reign in Jerusalem.

[19] After Jacob wrestled with God, Moses declared "Therefore, to this day the sons of Israel do not eat the sinew of the hip which is on the socket of the thigh." Is this a direct command of God? Perhaps not, but interesting nonetheless and illustrates the ancient nature of this aspect of *kosher* laws.

[20] Hegg, *Introduction to Torah Living*. TorahResource.com, 2002. pp. 188–189.

[21] See the *Mishnah*, tractate *Chullin*.

[22] I discovered way more information than I expected to when I researched the meat industry. An entire "rendering" industry processes 40 billion pounds of dead animals a year. After grinding and cooking, the mixture is separated into fatty matter (used in soaps, candles and cosmetics) and protein matter (used in livestock feed). See *Mad Cowboy* (Lyman), pages 11–12.

[23] Robbins, John. *Diet for a New America*. Stillpoint Publishing, 1987, pp. 107–110.

[24] Some retailers have their own standards for the meat they sell. For example, while Whole Foods Market's internal standards do not match certified organic standards, they do ensure that the meat they sell is free from hormones, antibiotics and animal by-products.

[25] According to the USDA, all fresh meat is considered "natural," even if it contains antibiotics and growth hormones.

[26] The federal guidelines for animal slaughter appear in Title 7, Chapter 48, Section 1902 of the U.S. Code.

[27] Regenstein, J.M. *Comprehensive Reviews in Food Science and Food Safety, Vol. 2*, 2003, p. 114.

[28] Colbert, p. 60

[29] Colbert, page 59. Besides the slaughter method, other aspects of the *kosher* meat laws result in more humane treatment of animals. For example, some inhumane methods of raising veal calves result in weak, sick animals that do not qualify for *kosher* status. See Rubenstein, *The Kashrus Manual*, pp. 72–73.

[30] Personal communication.

[31] Temple Grandin & Joe Regenstein, "Religious slaughter and animal welfare: a discussion for meat scientists." Meat Focus International, March 1994, pp. 115–123. Published by CAB International.

[32] Zechariah 9:7. While the context of Zechariah was partially fulfilled by Alexander the Great, its future fulfillment awaits for Messiah's return. See Keil & Delitzsch's *Commentary on the Old Testament* on this verse.

[33] See the Resources section on pages 147 and 148 for places to buy meat that has been raised and slaughtered biblically.

[34] Isaiah 2:3, Micah 4:2

Meat and Milk
Did My Ancestors Take it Too Far?

Lest my Jewish friends and family become smug at my challenge to Christians, I need to address my Jewish ancestors' long-held beliefs about avoiding meat and dairy combinations. Returning to the question I pondered after my lunch with Elizabeth, does God care if we eat today's beef chili in yesterday's cereal bowl? Here is what the Bible says about mixing meat and dairy:

> You shall not boil a young goat in its mother's milk. (Exodus 23:19, 34:26, Deuteronomy 14:21)

That's it. That's all the Torah says. Nothing else.

This command appears in the Torah three times, signaling that God takes it seriously. Thankfully, most of us can easily say that we regularly obey it. Very few of us boil young goats, let alone boil them in milk, let alone boil them in their mother's milk.

Picket Fence or Great Wall of China?

The biblical command not to boil a kid in its mother's milk has actually spawned a myriad of related rules. Modern-day observant Jews who practice meat and dairy separation (one aspect of "keeping *kosher*" introduced in chapter five) go beyond avoiding cheeseburgers. Current meat/dairy dietary fences[1] might include kitchens stocked with two sets of dishes, silverware, pots and pans. Some might even have separate sinks and dishwashers. These precautions reach so high that they guarantee that the follower will never accidentally boil a kid in mom's milk.

While these traditions may seem puzzling, I have learned from my unfolding journey that logical reasoning and Scripture itself often stand behind traditions that initially seem strange. I have also learned that many people find these traditions to be life-giving, so I want to respect them, even if I view them differently.

The Origins of Meat/Dairy Separation*

Most believers ascribe little if any authority to the traditional interpretation of the verse that says, "You shall not boil a young goat in its mother's milk." (Exodus 23:19) Regardless of our opinions, let's try to understand the traditional perspective. The interpretation of separating meat-foods from dairy-foods goes all the way back to the time of Jesus. Early Jewish literature records a dispute over the issue between two prominent schools of Pharisees—a full generation before Jesus.[2]

We do not know to what extent or stringency such separation was practiced in Jesus' day. Things had certainly not yet evolved to the point of separating dishes, kitchens or silverware. The same table could contain both meat and cheese, as long as the two were not eaten together. We do know that second-century Aramaic translations of the Bible translated the words, "do not boil a kid in its mother milk" as simply "do not eat meat in milk." Even in the days of the *Talmud* (approximately the fifth century), some Rabbis did not extend the prohibition of meat and milk to fowl, since chickens do not produce milk. Since those days, however, Judaism has reclassified poultry as "meat" for purposes of meat/dairy separation.

Some believers who choose to follow the Jewish traditions of separating meat and dairy point to the Master's declaration that "The scribes and the Pharisees have seated themselves in the chair of Moses; therefore all that they tell you, do and observe ..." (Matthew 23:2–3)

While the conventional rabbinic interpretation of the passage certainly seems excessive, most Christians reject all of it out of hand as unreasonable and unfounded within the laws of the Bible.

But despite my own misgivings, I (Lancaster) must admit the interpretation is not completely unreasonable. We similarly derive other broader laws based upon specific examples given in Bible.

For example, the law regarding an ox that gores (Exodus 21:28–29) establishes a principle for all similar cases of negligence, not just those cases involving oxen. Much like our modern-day "case law" or "common law" that establishes precedents for different cases with similar facts, the Bible often gives particular examples to illustrate a general command. Since it was common to eat goats and drink their milk in biblical times, the mainstream Jewish interpretation understood the particular example of a "kid in its mother's milk" to communicate a general ban on eating meat with milk together. In those days, bovine dairy was not generally consumed. Goat milk was dairy, and goat meat was the most common meat.

Examine the simple logic:

1. What is the purpose of cooking a goat in milk? Obviously, the intent for cooking something is to eat it. Therefore, it would seem that this is a prohibition mainly in regard to dietary laws.
2. If it wasn't a goat in goats' milk, but a calf in cows' milk, would it be any different? It must be, then, the mixture of meat with milk that this law addresses.
3. Therefore, Judaism does not eat any mixture of milk and meat, nor prepare it for others.

In conclusion, a prohibition on cooking meat and milk together, or perhaps simply eating them together, might be derived from the Bible, but the precise intention of the passage remains uncertain and open for debate.

* Many thanks to D. Thomas Lancaster for writing *The Origins of Meat/Dairy Separation*.

Other Theories behind Meat/Dairy Separation

Since the kid-in-its-mother's-milk verse is grouped with commands about sacrifice, Sabbath and the biblical festivals, the Sages presumed that the penalty for breaking it was severe. Therefore, creating such tall fences protected the people from incurring the penalty for an inadvertent violation.[3]

The *Life Application Study Bible* provides two additional theories, although these are pure speculation:

> This prohibition against cooking a young goat in its mother's milk may reflect a Canaanite fertility rite. Or it may just mean that the Israelites were not to take what was intended to promote life and use it to kill or destroy life.[4]

From a pure health perspective, Dr. Rex Russell validates the simple mandate to avoid eating meat and dairy products together. He observes that the practice makes sense, since milk's presence in the stomach inhibits meat's digestion when the two are eaten together.[5]

While not specifically directed by the written Word, avoiding eating meat and dairy products together may provide an added health benefit: It forces one to eat a greater quantity of life-giving Genesis 1:29 foods. Plant-based foods like grains, beans, fruit and vegetables are considered *pareve* (neutral) and therefore permitted at all meals.[6] Since science repeatedly tells us to incorporate more of these low-cost, high-nutrient, plant-based foods into our diets, maybe meat/dairy dietary separation is not such a bad idea after all.

Concluding Thoughts

While I am not comfortable with most details of modern meat/dairy separation, I am relieved to see that there was originally a certain logic to it. I also recall how burdensome it felt to adopt a Christian lifestyle (for example, avoiding raunchy movies or cussing) before I was compelled to embrace it. Afterwards, the previously restrictive lifestyle became second nature to me. Perhaps this is the experience of those who live out this verse according to today's Orthodox Jewish standards.

In fact, Jesus was not against traditions, and the New Testament has many references to His following traditions of that day. (His statements against certain ones were narrowly focused on those that negate the clear commands of Scripture.) In following Jesus' example regarding traditions, we would do well to incorporate those that help us remember the biblical commandments themselves—and avoid those that negate biblical commands.

Finally, our father Abraham not only appears to have served meat and dairy together, it seems that he served the combination to God, too.

> Now the LORD appeared to him [Abraham] ... while he was sitting at the tent door in the heat of the day. When he lifted up his eyes and looked, behold, three men were standing opposite him; and when he saw them, he ran from the tent door to meet them and bowed himself to the earth, and said, "My Lord, if now I have found favor in Your sight, please do not pass Your servant by ..." Abraham ... ran to the herd, and took a tender and choice calf and gave it to the servant, and he hurried to prepare it. He took curds and milk and the calf which he had prepared, and placed it before them ... (Genesis 18:1–3, 7–8)

From a plain reading of these few verses, Abraham did not practice the separation of meat and milk, and apparently neither did God Himself![7]

Most believers ascribe little, if any, authority to Judaism's current interpretation of this command. However, we all need to come to our own conclusions on the matter.

Questions to discuss and ponder

1. What does God say about eating meat and milk together?
2. How do current-day Orthodox Jews apply this command to their daily lives? How might this command originally have been understood?
3. What are some of the theories behind the meat/dairy separation?
4. What might some benefits of meat/dairy separation be? Some drawbacks?
5. If you do not observe the modern-day interpretation of this command, have you ever encountered someone who did? What thoughts or feelings did you have? How might their observance be life-giving to them?

Endnotes

[1] Recall from chapter three that Jewish Sages erected fences around the Torah to keep people from inadvertently violating it.

[2] m.*Chullin* 8. However, as part of the review of this information for *Holy Cow!*'s second edition, I discovered that there are differing opinions about whether this tradition actually goes as far back as Jesus' time. See the Epilogue for more information.

[3] Hegg, *Introduction to Torah Living*, p. 194.

[4] Kantzer, Kenneth. *Life Application Study Bible*. Tyndale House Publishers, 2000 on Deut 14:21.

[5] Russell, p. 271

[6] Lubavitch Women's Cookbook Publications. *Body & Soul, A Handbook for Kosher Living*, 1989, p. 24.

[7] Tessler, p. 83. Per D. Thomas Lancaster: Traditional Judaism (Ma'am Loez) assumes that Abraham first served them curds, and by the time it would take for the calf to be slaughtered, butchered and cooked, the minimum time between milk and meat would be easily satisfied.

7

Conclusion

God's Word Does Not Change—and Neither Does the Physiology of Pork or Shellfish

This book is not about salvation. It is not about how to gain right standing with God. I write as a redeemed child of God who seeks to understand His will and apply His wisdom and ways in all areas of my life—including eating. This is a book about eating. Eating is something I do several times a day, every day. I already have a relationship with God, but I still have to eat. My goal here has been to offer answers to the many questions that I have heard over the last few years—not to provide a recipe for righteousness.

Vegetarianism

So where does this leave my vegetarian friends?

God allowed Noah to eat meat. He also gives us clear meat-eating guidelines in Leviticus 11. Eating meat was a central part of God's ancient worship system. And while our bodies are designed to digest mostly vegetable products, they are also designed to process meat. For these reasons I do not believe that "God doesn't want us to eat meat," as some Christian vegetarians suggest.

At the same time, I fully affirm the vegetarian assessment about today's meat industry, the terrible conditions that many animals experience, and the serious health impact that mistreated animals can have on the humans who eat them.[1] Today's animal atrocities are the result of fallen man's desire for profit and lack of concern for the animals or the environment. These poor conditions also result in unsafe meat products. For example, the use of growth hormones that infiltrate our meat and dairy products has likely contributed to the onset of early puberty in many children; the frequent use of antibiotics and pesticides is associated with increased cancer rates. Thankfully, some meat producers and processors have responded to the public's outcry for humanely raising and slaughtering animals and are producing safer meat.

The meat industry's condition, however, is not entirely its fault. Our collective sin of gluttony has resulted in insatiable appetites and swelling portion sizes that encourage cattle producers to rely on antibiotics and growth hormones. Simple economics tells us that if we continue to demand (and eat) more meat products than God supplies to us naturally, artificial means will be used to increase the supply.

Although I do not suggest we avoid meat entirely, many of us would do well to eat it in smaller portions and less often. Eating more vegetables, whole grains, beans, legumes, nuts and seeds is a healthy, economical alternative to meat eating that springs directly from Genesis 1:29. In the Garden of Eden, God's original diet plan emphasized these foods.

The Bottom Line

Both science and Scripture lead me to think that pork, shellfish and other unclean meats were not created by God to be eaten. For nearly 2,000 years, however, Christians—both non-Jewish *and* many Jewish believers in Jesus—have used a variety of New Testament Bible verses and theologies to explain why these laws have been "fulfilled" or are otherwise no longer applicable. As such, unclean meat is not only acceptable to eat, but pork is commonly eaten to celebrate Christian holidays.

Man Alive! There's More!
D. Thomas Lancaster provides a look back at Church history on pages 129–131.

Both the Old and New Testaments also indicate that eating blood is forbidden. While the Bible does not spell out how, exactly, to do this, Christians can learn from the observant Jewish community, which has respected this command since the days of the Tabernacle. While eating *kosher* meat is not necessarily the only way to avoid eating blood, the original goal of the *kosher* meat industry was submission to God's written Word. At the same time, my ancestors' desire to obey God's Word was so great that the command not to boil a kid in its mother's milk evolved into legislation that seems to exceed God's original intent. While helpful to my understanding, I believe that traditional Christian and Jewish resources may lead me astray if I rely on them too much.

Looking for a Sign

In my constant search for discernment, I often wish God would send me an e-mail to make His will clear to me. Perhaps you feel the same way. Do I accept the new job offer? Do I home school my children? How do I juggle all the activities that compete for my time? While His Word certainly provides general guidance for daily living, when it comes to concrete, black-and-white direction, God's Word only takes us so far. From there we must wrestle with the issues, rely on the counsel of others, and discern God's will by leaning on Him directly through prayer and meditation.

I am thankful that this is not the case with meat. The clarity of Leviticus 11 is refreshing to me, since it clearly announces God's will for my meat choices. However, because of society's influence, traditional church teaching, and my own self-will (and love for ribs), I initially resisted the plain meaning of those verses. Eventually, however, after renewing my mind with interpretations of Scripture like those contained in the *Man Alive! There's More!* section that follows, choosing to avoid pork and shellfish has become effortless.

Over the past few years I have come to believe that the Scripture cannot be broken[2] and that God established His statutes to last forever.[3] To be clear, there are certainly Torah commands whose literal application still puzzles me. Rather than dismiss them as antiquated, obsolete or "fulfilled," however, I now hold them with an open hand and prayerfully seek more information about how they might apply to me.[4]

Pizza, Grilled Cheese and God's Will

I have a simple goal. I want God's written Word to inform all aspects of my life. To do so, I obviously need teachers and scholars to help me gain a deeper understanding of the Bible. At the same time, I am skeptical of interpretations of it—either Jewish or Christian—that deviate too far from what is written. D. Thomas Lancaster summarizes why I have become passionate about understanding and attempting to live out God's instructions:

> Every commandment of Torah is spoken by the mouth of God. Each command is therefore holy and eternal. Whether or not a particular commandment seems to apply in our day is irrelevant. Human society may change, but God does not change. Every commandment is a distillation of His essence, a pure revelation of His person. The study of the commandments is the study of God. As soon as we begin to discard commandments, we have begun editing God.[5]

At the same time, the amount of information contained in the Hebrew Scriptures can become overwhelming, especially for those whose faith walk is young. I do not believe that God wants us to become so bogged down in the details that we lose sight of His two greatest commandments: loving God and loving our neighbor. The Bible is a love story between God and His people, and His main desire is for us to be reconciled to Him and to those around us.

As they raised me, my parents had two goals: to love me and to teach me to love others. But they did not ignore what I ate, since it was an integral part of loving me. Left to my own devices, I would have eaten only pizza and grilled cheese sandwiches. Thankfully, Mom had better ideas, and her annoying pleas to "eat your vegetables" contributed to my well-being. If Mom's wisdom for my food choices was good for me, how much more so is the wisdom that comes directly from the Creator of anatomy, botany and zoology? God's love for us is immeasurable, so He has carefully crafted both our bodies and the fuel for them.

When I read the Bible as a whole, I see a God who cares about the details of how we live our lives—including what we eat. Regardless of your conclusions, I hope that *Holy Cow!* has helped you find some clarity and peace around this issue, and that you are motivated to seek out God's will for how you eat. May God Himself provide you with guidance for your next steps.

May God Himself, the God of peace, sanctify you through and through. May your whole spirit, soul and body be kept blameless at the coming of our Lord Jesus Messiah. The One who calls you is faithful and He will do it. (1 Thessalonians 5:23–24, NIV)

Questions to discuss and ponder

1. If you believe that the Leviticus 11 food laws are no longer applicable, what is your main reason? If you think they still apply, what is your main reason, and to whom do you think they apply?
2. Do you think vegetarianism was God's original design for mankind? Why or why not? Do you think it's the best way to live today? Why or why not?
3. How do you discern God's will in your life? How does this relate to how you discern your meat and other food choices?
4. If you think the food laws still apply, how might this impact your study and possible application of God's other laws that you might have never considered?
5. How has this study impacted your view of God, His character and His love for you?

Endnotes

[1] See *Mad Cowboy* (Lyman), *Diet for a New America* (Robbins) or www.ChristianVeg.com for more information about these conditions. These issues are also addressed in the January, 2005 issue of *Consumer Reports*, pages 26–31. For faith-based perspectives on this topic, see *Judaism and Vegetarianism* (Schwartz) and *They Shall Not Hurt or Destroy: Animal Rights and Vegetarianism in the Western Religious Traditions* (Murti).

[2] John 10:35

[3] Psalm 119:152

[4] First Fruits of Zion's *Torah Club Volume Five* by D. Thomas Lancaster provides teachings about the Torah's specific commands and how they might apply to believers today.

[5] Lancaster, D.T. *Torah Club Volume Five*. First Fruits of Zion, 2004. p. 433.

Epilogue

Second Edition Update

In 2003 I wrote an 8-page paper for my friends at church. It was called "Why I Don't Eat Pork," and it was born out of a need to explain my eating habits to my Christian friends. Several years later, while working as an editor for First Fruits of Zion, I was asked to compile the writings of D. Thomas Lancaster that related to the Bible's food laws, especially those relating to the clean and unclean meats in Leviticus 11. In the process, I realized that the book we were trying to create needed an introduction, so I offered to write it.

I guess I had a lot to say. The next thing you know, the book morphed into *Holy Cow!* with me privileged to be the primary author. It was first published by First Fruits of Zion in 2005. Although it was certainly not the first book on biblical eating, it was unique in the territory it covered and the way it was addressed.

In 2006 my son was born, which began my slow drift away from First Fruits of Zion due to motherhood demands. My new areas of passion? God's design for parenting. Gardening. How to feed my family healthy and nutritious meals. I co-wrote and published the *What the Bible Says about Healthy Living Cookbook* (Heart of Wisdom, 2009), and I happily immersed myself in "life application." While I was not actively spreading *Holy Cow!*'s message, its content was still near and dear to me.

In 2011 First Fruits of Zion published a new book on the dietary laws entitled *Biblically Kosher: A Messianic Jewish Perspective on Kashrut*, written by Aaron Eby—a top-notch writer, scholar and a *mensch* (Yiddish for really great guy). While our books overlap to some degree, they answer decidedly different questions. In *Holy*

Cow! I am seeking to answer the question, "How do I discern what meats God has designed to be eaten?" Aaron seeks to answer the question, "What is the biblical basis for 'traditional' Jewish kosher laws, and how do those laws apply to believers?"

I am grateful to First Fruits of Zion for offering me the publication rights to reprint *Holy Cow!* and release this new edition. D. Thomas Lancaster kindly agreed to "bequeath" his section of *Holy Cow!* to me. We agreed that Heart of Wisdom (whose founder Robin Sampson is passionate about the Hebrew roots of Christianity and biblical health) was a better publishing fit for me, especially since Heart of Wisdom published my cookbook.

Here are a few of the significant changes I made to the Second Edition en route from First Fruits of Zion to Heart of Wisdom.

Did God Design Food to Harm Us?

In the new edition I omit my subtle suggestion that God possibly introduced meat-eating after the flood in order to shorten man's life expectancy.

In Genesis 6:3 God states that man's "days shall be one-hundred and twenty years." In biblical eating circles (especially vegetarian and vegan ones) it is common to hear the misconception that God is declaring man's life expectancy to be 120 years rather than the 800 to 900 years.

I think a better understanding of this passage is simply that there will be 120 years until the flood starts and mankind is nearly wiped out.

Jewish Tradition: A Hot Button

I have tweaked my language to be more respectful of Jewish tradition. In the years since *Holy Cow!* was originally written, I have repeatedly discovered how many traditions are actually biblically *derived*. This belief was enhanced in my reading of Aaron Eby's book *Biblically Kosher*.

That said, I do not believe that many of those traditions are biblically *mandated*, so I am not personally convicted to follow all of them. However, I have seen fruit in the lives of those who do. In addition, I have experienced fruit in my own family from participating in some of these rich, long-standing traditions—including ones possibly enjoyed by Jesus. I believe that we all implement some type of traditions in our lives; for me there is richness in using those of ancient origins that have been handed down from generations.

Most importantly, though, some of my original interpretations regarding tradition were misguided. My oversimplified belief that Jesus butted heads with the religious leaders of His day over the mere presence of complex, religious traditions is a common misconception born out of unfamiliarity (and therefore discomfort) with Jewish traditions.

The truth is, the complexity that the Oral Law provides to sincere, observant Jews is actually life-giving to many of them. I have witnessed this from my own Orthodox Jewish friends; "burdensomeness" is relative and cultural. For people raised in strictly observant Jewish homes and who truly love God, traditions that are "burdensome" to me are as light as a feather to them.

Chapter 6 Update: Meat and Milk

My Chapter 6 Update was originally going to include fascinating details about the tradition of separating meat and dairy that I learned in *Biblically Kosher*. There is much presented in that book that sheds light on the details and biblical background for the tradition.

Upon further research, however, I learned that some people believe that this tradition originated *after* Jesus' time, not before as D. Thomas Lancaster presents in this chapter.

Here is my layman's take on a very complex subject.

Lancaster's support for the notion that Jesus definitely separated meat and dairy comes from the *Mishnah*, tractate *Chullin* 8, which states:

> Every flesh it is prohibited to cook in milk, except for the flesh of fish and locusts. And it is prohibited to serve it up onto the table with cheese, except for the flesh of fish and locusts. He who vows from flesh is permitted the flesh of fish and locusts. Fowl goes up onto the table with cheese, but it is not eaten," the words of the House of Shammai. And House of Hillel say, "It does not go up, and it is not eaten." Said R. Yose, "This is one of the lenient rules of the House of Shammai and the strict rulings of house of Hillel."

Since both Hillel and Shammai lived before Jesus, Lancaster (and many other wise and learned scholars) conclude that this tradition originated before Jesus and therefore was fully present (in some form) in the Jewish community during His lifetime.

Other learned scholars, however, disagree. The other perspective is that just because Shammai and Hillel lived before Jesus did, it does not necessarily mean teachings ascribed to their "houses" did, since their schools of thought are considered to this day.

As such, my periodic musings about separating meat and dairy in my own life "because Jesus did it," have faded.

While my personal conviction to separate meat and dairy has lessened through my research, my appreciation for this tradition has actually increased.

How can that be?

In the last few years I have learned that in Judaism this tradition is just as important as avoiding eating soft-shelled crabs. I have met Orthodox Jews, Messianic Jews (who were raised Orthodox) and even nominally observant Jewish friends and relatives who speak about meat/dairy separation as though it came directly from God. Although I may disagree with their perspective, their heart connection with this deeply ingrained tradition is indisputable, so I am compelled to respect it.

In addition, realizing how most Jewish folks see this tradition makes me see that belittling it in any way is an enormous stumbling block for Jewish people considering Jesus as Messiah.

Finally, as we look forward to Messiah's return and the entire nation of Israel coming to faith in Messiah (see Zechariah 12, especially verses 10 through 14), I cannot help but wonder, will they be serving cheeseburgers in Jerusalem? Probably not.

Good News

Given my "life application" focus, one of my deepest desires for this edition was to provide resources for finding meat that has been both raised and slaughtered in a biblical manner. I happily share a few of these companies in the Resources section on pages 147 and 148. If you are searching for this type of meat, I hope you enjoy them on the road to eating biblically!

Part II
Man Alive! There's More!
By D. Thomas Lancaster

Contents

Welcome to *Man Alive! There's More!* Written by FFOZ Educational Director and Bible teacher D. Thomas Lancaster, *Man Alive!* delves further into some of the most challenging Scripture passages mentioned in the main part of this book. Fasten your seatbelts and get out your Bibles; this may be the richest Scripture study you have ever experienced.

Most of these commentaries have been adapted from D. Thomas Lancaster's *Torah Club Volume Four* (a 1,100-page commentary on the Gospels and Acts) and *Torah Club Volume Five* (a 1,400-page messianic commentary on the Torah, focusing on the applicability of the laws). To learn more about Torah Club, to download samples or to join, please visit *www.torahclub.org*.

Clean and Unclean	
Leviticus 11	97
Jesus Declared All Foods Clean	
Mark 7:1–23	103
Peter's Vision of the Sheet	
Acts 10	109
Nothing Is Unclean in Itself	
Galatians 2:10–15; 1 Corinthians 8–10 and Romans 14	115
Doctrine of Demons	
1 Timothy 4:1–5 and Colossians 2:18–23	123
A Look Back at Church History	129

Man Alive!

Clean and Unclean

There's More on Leviticus 11*

To better comprehend God's dietary laws, we need to learn the basic distinction between clean and unclean.

The Bible says that some animals are "clean" and some are "unclean." That's easy enough to understand. In Leviticus 11, these adjectives describe animals that have been designated by the Lord as either fit or unfit for human consumption. But what does it mean to designate something as "unclean"? What does it mean to say that it is "clean"? What happens if we become "unclean"?

Notions of "ritual purity" and "impurity" ("clean" and "unclean") are some of the hardest of all biblical concepts to grasp. The ideas of clean and unclean seem weird and remote in our Western context. At first, the whole thing appears to have nothing to do with believers or with Jesus. This is indeed hard stuff. At the same time, if we are confused, annoyed or bored with it, the problem is likely on our end (in this case, with me trying to communicate it to you). God created this system and codified it in His Word, regardless of our thoughts and feelings about it.

One reason this stuff is so hard is that it all relates to God's dwelling place on earth: the Tabernacle or Temple. That makes it difficult for us to understand, since there has not been such a place in almost 2,000 years.

Levitical impurity (or being "unclean") is the biblical concept that a person or object can be in a state that—by the Bible's law—prevents the person or object from interacting with the Tabernacle or Temple and its sacrifices.

The words "clean" and "unclean" are misleading, since they seem to imply something about general hygiene. This is not a sanitation issue. A ritually unclean animal is not dirtier than a clean animal, and you cannot make a ritually unclean animal clean by giving it a good, hot, soapy bath. It is equally wrong to suppose that "clean" and "unclean" refer to an animal's moral state. If animals did have any moral sense, horses would certainly have a higher moral standard than goats; yet the Bible says that horses are considered unclean, while goats are considered clean. In the same regard, an unclean animal such as a camel is no more shameful or morally bankrupt than a clean animal like a giraffe. People who work closely with camels may disagree, but the point is clear. Ritual impurity is completely different from physical cleanness, and it has nothing to do with intrinsic goodness or badness.

Instead, clean and unclean must be understood as purely ritual states. They have real application only in regard to the Tabernacle/Temple, the priesthood and the sacrifices. Here is what they mean:

> CLEAN: Something that is in a state of ritual cleanness is fit for entering the sacred precinct of the Tabernacle/Temple of God, for sacrifice on the altar, and/or for contacting the Tabernacle/Temple's sacred elements.

> UNCLEAN: Something that is unclean is in a state of ritual defilement. This renders it unfit for entering the sacred precinct of God's Tabernacle/Temple, for sacrifice on the altar, and/or for contacting the Tabernacle/Temple's sacred elements.

Therefore, clean animals are regarded as fit for sacrificing. Unclean animals are not regarded as fit for sacrificing. Since we believers do not have a real, physical Temple in which we worship today, and since there is no sacrificial system today, most of the Bible's complex laws of clean and unclean have no real practical application in modern life. Levitical concerns about contracting ritual impurity through bodily discharges, dead rodents and lepers are not relevant without a Temple. Leviticus 11, however, does not directly address whether eating unclean animals will make you unclean or not. It simply forbids eating them.

Explaining the intricacies of the Tabernacle/Temple system, and the associated requirements for entering into God's presence in His dwelling place on earth, is beyond the scope of this book. I am making some sweeping generalizations about that system and its God-given requirements that may lead to more questions than answers. In fact, many of these generalizations may contradict what most of us have learned over the years about clean and unclean and the role of the Temple/Tabernacle. That makes sense. In order to read the Bible without getting stuck, this extremely detailed topic has, over the years, been understandably oversimplified.

As we study what the Bible says about eating meat, however, let's stick our toes into the deep ocean of meaning hidden beneath the surface of these concepts. Remember, if this topic confuses, annoys, repulses or bores us, the problem is with our lack of understanding—not with God's holy and perfect Word. But take heart. While the laws of clean and unclean do contain deep and profound spiritual lessons about separating the Kingdom of Light from the Kingdom of Darkness, we need not worry about practicing the non-eating-related instructions unless a Temple is rebuilt in Jerusalem and we plan to visit it.

Clean and Unclean: Not a Salvation Thing

As we begin to understand a tiny bit about clean and unclean, I hope two things are becoming clear.

First, becoming unclean is not a sin. A woman having her monthly period (Leviticus 15:25) and a woman who has just given birth (Leviticus 12:2) are both considered unclean by Levitical standards, but they obviously have not sinned. Think about it. If becoming unclean was truly a sin, Jesus would not have qualified as our perfect atoning sacrifice. Why? He deliberately touched dead people (Luke 7:14) and lepers (Matthew 8:3, Mark 1:41). According to the Torah, both of these actions would have rendered Jesus unclean and temporarily ineligible to participate in Temple worship activities. However, since the Living Word (Jesus) had perfect understanding of and unity with God's Written Word (the Bible, that is, Torah), He knew that becoming unclean was not the same thing as sinning. He healed the leper and raised the dead with His touch, not in defiance of the Torah's rules, but in conformity with them.

Second, the Bible's designation of when someone was unclean had nothing to do with the person's right-standing before God. It was simply part of God's system for designating who was eligible to enter His physical dwelling place on earth (the Tabernacle/Temple). It had nothing to do with salvation, justification or righteousness before God. Remember that righteousness has always come by faith, before, during and since Tabernacle/Temple times. (See chapter one, under the section, "Did Torah Justify God's People?") The New Testament reminds us that "it is impossible for the blood of bulls and goats to take away sins." (Hebrews 10:4) Rather, the blood of the Temple/Tabernacle sacrificial system provided a covering for sin so that man could approach God in His earthly home.

Eternal right-standing before God has always come through faith. Sacrifices in the earthly Tabernacle/Temple both foreshadowed Messiah's eternal sacrifice, and they provided a way for humans to interact with God on earth.

What does all of this have to do with eating? Nothing! That's the point! We highlight the basics of the Temple/Tabernacle system to avoid the temptation of skimming Leviticus 11, seeing the words "clean" and "unclean," and dismissing the whole chapter—including the food laws—as irrelevant.

The careful reader sees that Leviticus 11 addresses two different things. First, God shows how to avoid becoming unclean (by not touching certain carcasses). This enables a person to enter the Tabernacle/Temple and make sacrifices. Indeed, this is not applicable today, since there is no earthly Temple/Tabernacle. Second, He tells His people which animals are permissible to eat. This is unrelated to one's ability to participate in the sacrificial system.

Just as He forbids us from offering unclean animals upon His altar, so too He forbids us from taking unclean animals into the Temple of our bodies. This is relevant for anyone looking to the Scriptures for food-choice guidance.

With this theory in mind, go back and reread Leviticus 11. Notice the different language used for food commands ("you may eat ..." "you must not eat ...") and those related to the Temple/Tabernacle system ("whoever touches their carcasses will be unclean till evening ..."). Also notice that when a person becomes unclean by touching a dead rodent or some other nasty thing, it is only a temporary condition, usually lasting only until sunset. The Bible provides rituals, like immersion in water, so the unclean person may be declared clean again, enter God's Temple, and participate in the worship. On the other hand, an unclean animal will always be unclean. There is no ritual that can ever make it clean. The Torah does not provide a remedy for a person who eats unclean animals, just as it does not provide a remedy for someone who gives false testimony or covets his neighbor's wife. They are all actions that God simply forbids. Even though God forgives those who repent from lying or envying, it does not mean that we endorse those behaviors, does it?

These seemingly bizarre concepts may baffle us, but remember: they are part of God's Word. God Himself created and designed the entire sacrificial system and its associated laws. And since Jesus Himself did not seem to have a problem with this system,[1] we would do well to be cautious about dismissing it.

* Written by both D. Thomas Lancaster and Hope Egan.

Man Alive!

Jesus Declared All Foods Clean

There's More on Mark 7:1–23

Jesus declared all foods clean. That seems obvious enough from Mark chapter seven and its parallels. After all, Mark 7:19 states the matter very succinctly: "Thus He declared all foods clean." Therefore, anyone prompting Christians to reconsider the Hebrew Scriptures' laws of clean and unclean meats would seem to be sadly misinformed. If Jesus declared all foods clean, who are we to say that pork or even camel meat is unclean?

But there are some quandaries with our traditional reading of Mark seven. First, how can Jesus legitimately declare all foods clean when His heavenly Father has said that we are to distinguish between clean and unclean meats? Can Jesus topple the laws of the Father? Wouldn't that be a contradiction?

There are more problems. If He did declare that all foods are clean, He would disqualify Himself as Messiah because His teaching would be contrary to the written Word of God. The Bible says that a legitimate King of Israel is not to depart from the Law of God either to the right or to the left.[2] Toppling the laws of Leviticus 11 would certainly be a big left turn. His opponents among the Pharisees would have all the evidence that they needed to impugn Him without any further inquiry. "This man is not from God; He teaches against the laws of God."

Finally, the Greek manuscripts of the book of Mark do not actually contain the words, "Thus He declared all foods clean." Check your trusty old King James Version of Mark 7:19. It reads quite differently.

Let's take a fresh look at the passage in its full context.

The Delegation from Jerusalem

The Sanhedrin had heard enough reports about the prophet from Galilee that they decided to investigate. Their job was to determine if Jesus was a legitimate man of God or if He was a heretic. Deuteronomy 13:4–5 warns about any prophet who might preach "rebellion against the LORD your God" or try to "seduce you from the way in which the LORD your God commanded you to walk." According to that passage, any man claiming to speak on God's behalf and teaching against the commandments of God was to be put to death.

The Sanhedrin wanted to ascertain if Jesus (who appeared to be a prophet) spoke and acted in accordance with God's Word or not. If they determined that He was teaching against the Torah or in contradiction to the commandments, then they were obligated to expose Him as a false prophet and prosecute Him. As the guardians of the faith, that was their job.

Unwashed Hands

Upon arriving in the Galilee, the delegation found Jesus and His disciples breaking bread and eating. The Pharisees immediately observed that the disciples did not perform a ritual hand washing before eating. They must have wondered about this. If this were really a prophet or the Messiah, wouldn't He have taught His disciples regarding the uncleanness of the hands?

The custom of ritual hand washing before handling and eating food was a Pharisaic tradition, but it was not a commandment of the Scriptures. It belonged to the legislation of the Oral Torah, allegedly received from Moses at Mount Sinai. An entire section of the *Mishnah* (part of the Oral Torah) is dedicated to the subject of ritual hand washing. Although proven valuable in basic hygiene, the requirement to wash one's hands before eating is not a biblical commandment.

The reasoning behind ritual hand washing can be derived from the Bible. In the Bible, human beings can become unclean or even ritually contaminating.[3] For example, someone who has touched a corpse becomes not only unclean, but anything he touches will also be rendered contaminated.[4] In addition, we have seen that the Bible specifies that the meat of certain animals is unclean and therefore forbidden for consumption, whereas other meats are clean and are therefore permissible.

The Oral Torah took these basic Bible concepts and combined them for what might be a logical conclusion: that touching bread with unclean hands rendered the bread unclean. According to this idea, an unclean person handling otherwise clean food renders that food unclean and therefore forbidden for consumption. Thus if you were unclean (for whatever reason) and went to eat a peanut-butter sandwich with ritually unclean hands, that sandwich would be rendered ritually unclean by your touch. Suddenly the peanut-butter sandwich would be almost as unclean as a ham sandwich. Remember though, this is all inferred. It is not stated anywhere in the Bible. It is a matter of Pharisaic tradition.

The Pharisees took it very seriously and added more than a little superstition to it as well. For example, the *Talmud* in tractate *Yoma* speaks of an evil spirit that clings to people's hands until they are ritually washed. Consider the following excerpts from the *Talmud*:

> Anyone who does not wash his hands before he eats bread is as unclean as if he had had sex with a prostitute, as it is written, "for the prostitute reduces you to a loaf of bread." (b.*Sotah* 4b citing Proverbs 6:26)
>
> Rabbi Zerika said in the name of Rabbi Eleazar, "Whoever disregards the washing of hands before a meal will be uprooted from the world ..." Rabbi Abbahu says, "Whoever eats bread without first washing his hands is as though he eats unclean food; as it is written, 'In this way the people of Israel will eat defiled food.'" (b.*Sotah* 4b citing Ezekiel 4:13)

If these quotes at all represent the conviction of the Pharisees in Jesus' day, we understand their shock and disappointment that Jesus' disciples did not wash their hands according to the traditions of the elders. They would regard such an abrogation of the religious norm as a strike against Jesus' legitimacy.

Contradicting God's Commandments

But does the Bible really say that bread can be made unclean and contaminating by being handled with unwashed hands? No, it does not.

So they asked Jesus, "Why do Your disciples not walk according to the tradition of the elders, but eat their bread with impure hands?"

The Master replies with a quote from Isaiah that essentially classifies these ritual hand washings as "rules taught by men." That is to say they are not commandments of God; they are human innovations. Obsession with ritual minutia can be a substitute for genuine faith and obedience. He tells them that in their pursuit of ritual purity they have neglected the legitimate commandments of God: "Neglecting the commandment of God, you hold to the tradition of men." He also told them, "You are experts at setting aside the commandment of God in order to keep your tradition."

But washing one's hands before eating seems like a harmless enough tradition. How could it contradict the command of God?

In Leviticus God commands: "You are to make a distinction between the unclean and the clean, and between the edible creature and the creature which is not to be eaten." (Leviticus 11:47) By declaring otherwise clean food to be unclean (simply because it had been touched by unwashed hands), the Pharisees were transgressing the commandment to correctly "make a distinction between the unclean and the clean." They were declaring what was fit for consumption to be unfit. They were declaring what was permissible to be forbidden, all on the basis of a tradition. In essence, the commandments of God that delineate between clean and unclean were being disregarded in favor of a tradition.

An Unclean Heart

Jesus goes on to declare to the crowd that nothing going into a man can make a person unclean; rather, what comes out of a man is what makes him unclean. When Jesus and the disciples were alone in the house, the disciples question Him about the teaching. They were perplexed by Jesus' words because they understood full well from biblical law that there are a variety of things a person can eat that render him unclean.[5]

After soundly rebuking the Pharisees for employing traditions that nullify the commandments of God, would Jesus Himself turn around and nullify Leviticus 11? No. The disciples misunderstood because they thought He was speaking literally. He was not. It was a parable. The text says so in Mark 7:17. Frustrated that they had taken Him literally and missed the larger point He was making, He asked them, "Are you so lacking in understanding also?" (Mark 7:18)

It is easy to see how the disciples lacked in understanding! Like them, we typically take the Master's words and apply them to Leviticus 11, as if that were the subject He was talking about. We mistakenly assume Jesus was speaking literally, and therefore He somehow overturned the laws of permissible and forbidden meats.

Jesus explains to His disciples that it is not ritual purity (clean and unclean) that He is concerned about; it is the uncleanness of the heart. He was not talking about actual Levitical purity at all except to use the purity framework to illustrate His point about the purity of a person's heart. Eating unclean food does not make a person's heart unclean. Whatever you eat passes through the system. It does not lodge in the heart (except maybe cholesterol). However, things that rise from within a person such as evil thoughts, sexual immorality, theft, murder, adultery, greed, malice, deceit, lewdness, envy, slander, arrogance and folly make the heart unclean.

Potty Talk

Thus nothing that enters a man from the outside can make him "unclean" where "unclean" means having an unclean heart. Eating unclean bread does not make a man's heart unclean. Instead, the Master points out that unclean bread "entereth not into his heart, but into the belly, and goeth out into the draught, purging all meats." (Mark 7:19 KJV) That is to say, it passes through the digestive system and goes out the end opposite from whence it came in. This is the plain meaning of the passage.

Yet some translators take the clause "purging all meats" as a narrator's parenthetical statement and translate "purging" as "Thus He declared all foods clean." The words "Thus He declared," however, are not in the Greek text. They are supplied by the translator to make the new construction of the sentence fit. The Greek text literally says, "purging all foods." Jesus was not setting aside the Law; He was talking about (*ahem*) "going potty."

Unclean Bread?

The NASB translation, for example, takes the clause as a parenthetical summary statement. As we have already noted, the old King James follows a more literal reading. But what if the parenthetical statement created by the translators is actually correct? Is it possible that Jesus, contrary to Torah, declared all foods clean?

The assumed parenthetical statement is often cited as the major proof for the belief that Jesus abrogated the dietary laws. The common belief is that as a result of Mark 7:19, we can now eat ham roasted in snail sauce.

But even if the phrase should be translated as a parenthetical statement, we must ask ourselves, "What is the context of Jesus' comments?" Were the disciples actually eating unclean food? They were not. When criticized by the Pharisees, they were eating bread. What does eating bread have to do with God's laws of clean and unclean meat? How can bread be unclean?

Jesus did not declare all foods clean; He did not contradict the Scriptures; and He is the legitimate King of Israel who did not depart from God's Law, neither to the right nor to the left.

Man Alive!

Peter's Vision of the Sheet

There's More on Acts 10

Did God show Peter that the prohibition on eating unclean animals was repealed by giving him the vision of the sheet let down from heaven? Many of us have been taught that God used Peter's dream in Acts 10 to authoritatively declare all animals clean and fit for consumption. This interpretation, however, has some flaws. The Bible does not say that at all. Neither does Peter. In fact, when we dig a little deeper, we discover that Peter interpreted the vision of the sheet quite differently. Our traditional "now all foods are clean" interpretation needs to be re-examined before we discover the real meaning of the vision. Let's take a closer look.

Misinterpreting the Vision

Simon Peter was staying at the house of Simon the Tanner in Joppa. Peter was up on the roof praying, probably to escape the nasty smell of the tanner's house. As a fisherman, Peter was accustomed to smelly occupations, but the ancient tanning trade was the worst of all. He was praying on the roof, and as he prayed, he fell into a vision.

In his vision, he saw a sheet let down from heaven containing both clean and unclean animals. He heard a voice say, "Get up, Peter, kill and eat!" (Acts 10:13) The vision of the sheet from heaven is usually interpreted to mean that the dietary laws in the Torah have been revoked. But this interpretation is not supported by the text.

First, this interpretation contradicts earlier Scripture. If we accept the traditional interpretation (that God intended for His people to disregard the laws of clean and unclean), then we must concede that God has changed His mind and repealed His eternal and unchanging Torah. We are left with Holy Scripture that hopelessly contradicts itself. The result of such thinking is that no Scripture is certain, and no mandate of God is definite.

A second problem with the "all foods clean" interpretation of Peter's vision is that it is only a vision. The conventional understanding seems to assume that Peter proceeded to kill and eat the animals in the sheet, enjoying a sumptuous feast of wild beasts, cats and lizards. In fact, Peter does not "kill and eat," but responds correctly and lawfully, "By no means, Lord!" After this happens two more times, the sheet is withdrawn.

In addition, the "all foods clean" interpretation ignores the literary antecedent of Ezekiel 4:11–15 where the prophet Ezekiel is called upon to eat bread made unclean from contact with human excrement. Like Peter, Ezekiel protests:

> Ah, Lord GOD! Behold, I have never been defiled; for from my youth until now I have never eaten what died of itself or was torn by beasts, nor has any unclean meat ever entered my mouth. (Ezekiel 4:14)

Just as God relents and allows Ezekiel to instead use cow manure for fuel, God relents in Peter's vision, where the sheet is withdrawn.

Furthermore, the "all foods clean" interpretation is not part of the story. Though there is discussion of eating with Gentiles, there is no mention of eating unclean animals before or after the vision. Neither is that interpretation born out by the remainder of Acts, which continues to paint the believers as a Torah-observant sect of Judaism.

Finally, and most importantly, the "all foods clean" interpretation contradicts Peter's own interpretation of the vision later in chapter 10 and again in chapter 11.

Despite these objections, Acts 10 is often taught as the Bible passage that made the meat laws obsolete. A careful reading, however, reveals that this passage does not suggest a change to the Torah's dietary prohibitions.

The Real Meaning of the Vision

The Bible does not leave us guessing about the real meaning of the vision. In Acts 10:28–29 Peter himself explains the meaning. Then in Acts 11:1–18 he explains it again to his colleagues in Jerusalem. Therefore our attempts to reinterpret the vision as a repealing of the biblical dietary laws is not only unwarranted, it is unbiblical.

Peter explains the vision as thus: "God has shown me that I should not call any *man* common or unclean." (Acts 10:28, emphasis mine) That is, one should not designate one group of human beings as ritually pure and another as ritually impure. The vision is not literally talking about eating or cannibalism. Instead, the clean and unclean animals were understood metaphorically to represent human beings.

Uncleanness and Gentiles

One of the stringencies of first-century Judaism was a prohibition on entering the homes of Gentiles and eating with Gentiles. Though we have little information on the exact nature of the prohibition, it is largely inferred from John 18:28, Acts 10:28 and Galatians 2:11–15. It seems to also be reflected in the *Mishnah* where we read, "The dwelling places of Gentiles are unclean." (m.*Oholot* 18:7)

The Torah of Moses contains no such law. There is not a biblical law forbidding Jews from mingling with or eating with Gentiles. There are prohibitions about eating idol sacrifices,[6] but God never forbade entering a Gentile home or eating with a Gentile. Those laws and traditions seem to have arisen as rabbinic fences to protect Jews from ritual contamination and cultural assimilation. According to mainstream Jewish interpretation (in first-century Israel) of the laws of clean and unclean, Gentiles were classified as unclean and to be avoided. Eating with them was discouraged; entering their homes was regarded as contaminating.

Until his vision, Peter's understanding was that as a Jew, he was not to associate with Gentiles, enter their homes, or eat with them. This had theological ramifications. If Gentiles were not even eligible for table-fellowship with Jews, how much less were they eligible for the Kingdom of Heaven!

But Peter's assumption was in error. Those prohibitions did not arise from the Bible, but only from the stringencies of men's interpretations. God had never designated Gentiles unclean,[7] nor had He declared their homes or foods defiling. Yet if invited to eat a meal at a Gentile home, the first-century Jew would be required to decline on the basis that the food was (theoretically) rendered unclean through contact with Gentiles, even if the meat they served was in line with Leviticus 11. So too, if invited into a Gentile's home, the first-century Jew would place himself into a state of assumed ritual impurity.

For these reasons, if not for the vision of the sheet, Peter would have refused the invitation to enter the home of Cornelius the Roman centurion. He also would have refused the notion that Gentiles could participate in the Kingdom of Heaven. The vision of the sheet is offered as corrections on both of these points.

Distinguishing between Clean and Unclean

As the sheet is let down from heaven, Peter sees that it is full of both clean and unclean animals. He is instructed to "kill and eat." He refuses, saying, "By no means, Lord, for I have never eaten anything unholy and unclean." (Acts 10:14) Peter's response to the heavenly voice is correct. He refuses to "kill and eat" unclean animals on the basis that God has already declared the unclean animals unfit for consumption. Therefore the voice answers, "Do not call anything common that God has made clean." Perhaps the inverse is also true: "Do not call anything clean that God has made unclean."

Peter has correctly distinguished between clean and unclean, refusing to eat the unclean on the basis that God Himself designated categories of clean and unclean animals. How then, would Peter dare to call something common and unclean that God has declared clean, namely human beings cleansed by faith? The message is essentially, "You have rightly distinguished between clean and unclean animals on the basis of My authority; now receive the Gentiles as clean on the basis of My authority." As Peter explains, "God has shown me that I should not call any *man* common or unclean." (Acts 10:28, emphasis mine) Notice that he does not say, "God has shown me that I should not call any *thing* unclean." As

Peter understood the vision, it was a correction of the tradition-based prohibition on Jews mixing with Gentiles—not an alteration of the biblical prohibition on consuming unclean animals.

God Explains the Vision

The vision's meaning was not immediately clear to Peter. Acts 10:17 tells us that Peter was greatly perplexed as to what the vision might be. He clearly did not understand the vision to mean that all meats had suddenly been declared fit to eat. He was still wondering about what it meant when the Gentiles sent by Cornelius arrived at the house. He could hear them calling out, "Is this the house where Simon called Peter is staying?" Suddenly the Spirit of the Lord moved and spoke to him, explaining the vision, "Behold, three men are looking for you. But get up, go downstairs and accompany them without misgivings, for I have sent them Myself." (Acts 10:19–20) Now the meaning of the vision was clear. He was not to regard these Gentiles as unclean. He was to have no hesitation about traveling with them, eating with them or entering their homes. In other words, God was instructing him to receive the non-Jewish believers—not pork and shellfish—as clean.

Man Alive!

Nothing Is Unclean in Itself

There's More on Galatians 2:10–15;
1 Corinthians 8–10 and Romans 14

Does Paul oust the biblical dietary laws in Romans 14:14 where he says that "nothing is unclean in itself"? In direct contradiction to whole chapters of the Bible, does he teach us that we can eat whatever we want and ignore the biblical dietary laws? After all, he is convinced that "nothing is unclean in itself," unless a person thinks that it is unclean.

But what if we were to apply this logic to God's other commandments? Suppose we were to say, "Nothing is idolatry unless we think it is idolatry," or, "It's not adultery unless you think its adultery," or "It's not murder unless you think it's murder." These are obviously ridiculous examples. The point is that no man—not even Paul—can suddenly nullify or alter Bible commands. Paul is not a proponent of subjective morality. So how can he say that "nothing is unclean in itself"? The answer requires us to take a fascinating journey into the laws and scruples of first-century Judaism.

Rebuking Peter

While examining Peter's vision of the sheet, we learned that one of the stringencies of first-century Judaism was a prohibition on eating with Gentiles, whether in their homes or from food that was prepared by them. But we saw that the Torah contains no laws forbidding Jews from mingling with or eating with Gentiles. While there are prohibitions against eating idol sacrifices,[8] God never forbade Jews from entering a Gentile's home or eating with a Gentile. Again, those laws and traditions seem to have arisen as rabbinic fences to protect Jews from the possibility of ritual contamination or assimilation.

One of the concerns stemmed from the likelihood that Gentile food had been offered, in part, to an idol. To avoid that possibility, traditionalist Jews discouraged eating with Gentiles, entering their homes, or eating their food.

We saw that Peter's vision of the sheet was meant to squash these taboos. It was not meant to overturn the biblical dietary laws; it was a correction to the stringencies regarding Gentiles. The vision was meant to remove any reluctance that Peter might have harbored regarding traveling to Caesarea, entering the home of Cornelius, and presenting the Gospel.

Paul reports that, while in Antioch, Peter was still not completely settled on the issue of eating with Gentiles. The story of Paul's confrontation with Peter in Antioch is retold in Galatians 2:11–14.

> But when Cephas came to Antioch, I opposed him to his face, because he stood condemned. For prior to the coming of certain men from James, he used to eat with the Gentiles; but when they came, he began to withdraw and hold himself aloof, fearing the party of the circumcision. The rest of the Jews joined him in hypocrisy, with the result that even Barnabas was carried away by their hypocrisy. But when I saw that they were not straightforward about the truth of the gospel, I said to Cephas in the presence of all, "If you, being a Jew, live like the Gentiles [i.e., eating with Gentiles] and not like the Jews, how is it that you compel the Gentiles to live like Jews?" (Galatians 2:11–14)

The Jewish customs Paul referred to (when he referred to living "like Jews") were the rabbinic traditions forbidding Jews to eat with Gentiles. In the home-setting of the early congregations, where the breaking of bread was a regular part of meeting and worshipping together, such scruples meant a complete separation between Jewish and Gentile believers. Peter "lived like a Gentile" in as much as he freely fellowshipped with and ate with Gentiles subsequent to his vision in Acts 10. Under the influence of "certain men from James," however, Peter apparently reconsidered that decision.

A similar question of table-fellowship between Jewish and Gentile believers lies behind the vexing questions of Romans 14. The man of weak faith who eats only vegetables is most likely the traditionalist Jew who will not eat meat or wine (though it is biblically fit to eat) from a Gentile table. The man of strong faith who eats everything is the Jew who has accepted the Apostolic ruling that otherwise biblically fit foods are not made "common" (and therefore forbidden) simply because they have been prepared by Gentiles or because they were in the possession of Gentiles.

To this day, traditional Orthodox Judaism holds that food prepared by a Gentile without Jewish supervision is not to be regarded as fit for eating, even if it is otherwise biblically fit food.

Food Rendered Unclean by Idols

There is a real, biblical law that forbids us to partake of food that has been sacrificed to an idol. Exodus 34:15 says, "otherwise you might make a covenant with the inhabitants of the land and they would play the harlot with their gods and sacrifice to their gods, and someone might invite you to eat of his sacrifice."

While the context of this law was clearly an injunction against practicing idolatry, in first-century Judaism this verse was also understood as a prohibition on consuming anything, whether food or drink, that had been offered to an idol or "polluted by idols." Whether or not it was permissible to eat meat that had been sacrificed to idols was a divisive issue among first-century believers. Paul devotes a considerable amount of discussion to this issue in his letters. But the question is less straightforward than we might imagine. A closer examination of the first-century situation, and a comparison with the contemporary Jewish sources, reveals layers of complexity that the modern reader could scarcely guess. This issue is neither well-understood nor often discussed, since it is largely a moot point. When we buy meat from the modern supermarket, we never concern ourselves with whether or not it has been sacrificed to an idol. Yet in the days of the Apostles, this was a real concern. Meat bought in the marketplace of Corinth or Ephesus or any Diaspora city was very likely the prime cuts from a temple sacrifice earlier that morning or leftovers from an idolatrous ritual-feast enjoyed the previous night. The first drawing of each vat of wine made by Gentile wine makers was almost certainly poured out to the Greek god of wine. According to conventional Jewish norms, that first libation rendered the rest of the wine in the vat as "offered to an idol" and unfit for consumption.

Almost all of the arguments and questions over food and drink and eating with Gentiles arise from the concern around food sacrificed to idols. When removed from that context, the modern reader misinterprets these passages by assuming the argument was over the eating of clean or unclean animals.

In first-century Judaism, there was a deep concern with food sacrificed to idols. Partaking of food or drink that had been offered to a pagan god was expressly forbidden. Even among the believers, this was never sanctioned. Acts 15:20 forbids even the Gentile believers from eating things polluted by idols. In the book of Revelation, Jesus rebukes two congregations for compromising on this and eating food sacrificed to idols.[9]

The Difference between Common and Unclean

In Jewish estimation, any food that had been offered to an idol or as part of an idolatrous feast was regarded as "common." The Greek word is *koinos*. It means common, vulgar or profane. This is not the same as saying that it was ritually unclean in the biblical sense. The Greek word for biblically, ritually unclean is *akathartos*. The Septuagint, the Greek version of the Hebrew Scriptures, translates ritual uncleanness as *akathartos*. It is critical that we understand the difference between these two Greek words.

> KOINOS: Common. When used in reference to traditional Jewish dietary law, it refers to otherwise biblically fit food that man or tradition has rendered unfit for consumption.

> AKATHARTOS: Unclean. When used in reference to Jewish dietary law, it refers to the meats that the Bible has declared unclean and forbidden.

The word *koinos* (common) does not refer to impurity as defined by the Torah. The word *koinos* is reserved to apply to things made unfit through contact with idolatry or with Gentiles. Therefore, in Greek, pork would be *akathartos*. Wine poured out to an idol would be *koinos*.

Food Sacrificed to Idols

The believers did have concerns about food being rendered *koinos*. Though some among the Corinthian believers thought that meat sacrificed to idols should be permissible to them,[10] Paul sternly warns them against knowingly eating food sacrificed to idols. He warns them that to do so would create a stumbling block[11] for weaker brothers. He warns them to "flee from idolatry," (1 Corinthians 10:14) and to refuse to eat any food that was certainly offered to an idol.[12]

On the other hand, Paul concedes that one need not be overly concerned about whether food in the meat market was sacrificed to idols or not. He says, "Eat anything that is sold in the meat market without asking questions for conscience' sake; 'for the Earth is the LORD's, and all it contains.'" (1 Corinthians 10:25–26 quoting Psalm 24:1) Paul's point is that he eats unto the Lord, not unto an idol. "If I partake with thankfulness, why am I slandered concerning that for which I give thanks? Whether, then, you eat or drink or whatever you do, do all to the glory of God." (1 Corinthians 10:30–31) In other words, as long as he does not know that it was offered to an idol, he assumes it was not. Instead he eats it unto the Lord. It is akin to a "Don't ask, don't tell" policy, quite the opposite of the stringent rigidity that traditional Judaism prescribed for the matter.

Yet Paul does not go so far as to sanction intentional eating of meat sacrificed to idols. He warns the Corinthians not to eat with an idolater,[13] so too he warns the Ephesians not to partake with idolaters.[14] He reminds the Corinthians that the table of idols is the table of demons.

> No, but I say that the things which the Gentiles sacrifice, they sacrifice to demons and not to God; and I do not want you to become sharers in demons. You cannot drink the cup of the Lord and the cup of demons; you cannot partake of the table of the Lord and the table of demons. (1 Corinthians 10:20–21)

In the end, Paul's attitude toward meat sacrificed to idols was one of caution. He forbade his congregants from intentionally partaking in food sacrificed to idols, but he steered them away from being overly suspicious, which would ban them from eating meat from the market or in the homes of unbelievers. He reminds us that "food will not commend us to God; we are neither the worse if we do not eat, nor the better if we do eat." (1 Corinthians 8:8)

Nothing Is Unclean?

Paul does not take a hard stand on the issue of foods that have only potentially been offered to an idol. The conservatives in Rome certainly considered foods prepared by Gentiles as *koinos* (common) because they were potentially defiled by idolatry. Rather than eat meat or drink wine that might have been associated with idolatry and thereby rendered *koinos*, those conservatives chose to refrain from meat and wine and ate only vegetables as Daniel did in Babylon. Paul regards this as a debatable matter and leaves it to the conscience of the individual.

> One person has faith that he may eat all things, but he who is weak eats vegetables only. The one who eats is not to regard with contempt the one who does not eat, and the one who does not eat is not to judge the one who eats, for God has accepted him. Who are you to judge the servant of another? To his own master he stands or falls; and he will stand, for the Lord is able to make him stand. (Romans 14:2–4)

Though he advocates tolerance of those who insist on regarding meat and drink potentially defiled by idolatry as *koinos*, he himself is convinced that no food is *koinos*. He says as much in Romans 14:14:

> I know and am convinced in the Lord Jesus that nothing is unclean (*koinos*) in itself; but to him who thinks anything to be unclean (*koinos*), to him it is unclean (*koinos*). (Romans 14:14)

Unfortunately, this passage is almost universally misapplied to laws of clean and unclean animals as if Paul said that "nothing is unclean (*akathartos*) in itself." He did not. He did not use the Greek equivalent for "unclean," he used the equivalent for "common." There is a huge difference between the two. His statement that "nothing is unclean in itself" is completely unrelated to the laws of clean and unclean animals. It is a question of whether or not food is permissible when it might potentially have been offered to an idol.

As in Corinthians, he warns his readers not to let their liberal interpretation of food sacrificed to idols become a stumbling block to others.

> Do not tear down the work of God for the sake of food. All things indeed are clean, but they are evil for the man who eats and gives offense. It is good not to eat meat or to drink wine, or to do anything by which your brother stumbles. (Romans 14:20–21)

Notice that in this passage he mentions wine as one of the questionable foods. Biblical dietary laws never speak of unclean wine. Wine is a *koinos* issue, not a clean/unclean issue. Paul is definitely speaking about the issue of food potentially rendered *koinos* by contact with Gentiles and/or idolatry. Unfortunately, when passages like Romans 14 and 1 Corinthians 8–10 are taken out of their first-century Jewish matrix, we misunderstand them and assume that they are sanctioning the consumption of unclean meats forbidden by the Torah. Once again, it is man-made laws—not God's laws—that are being addressed.

Man Alive!

Doctrine of Demons

There's More on 1 Timothy 4:1–5 and Colossians 2:18–23

In his first letter to Timothy, Paul warns him of the "doctrine of demons" that forbids marriage and that commands abstinence from certain foods.

> But the Spirit explicitly says that in later times some will fall away from the faith, paying attention to deceitful spirits and doctrines of demons, by means of the hypocrisy of liars seared in their own conscience as with a branding iron, men who forbid marriage and advocate abstaining from foods which God has created to be gratefully shared in by those who believe and know the truth. For everything created by God is good, and nothing is to be rejected if it is received with gratitude; for it is sanctified by means of the word of God and prayer. (1 Timothy 4:1–5)

Some of us have misunderstood this passage to mean that the Torah's dietary laws are a "doctrine of demons." This is an impossible interpretation for a number of reasons. It is blasphemous to regard the commandments of God as the doctrines of demons. Paul himself observed the Torah, including Leviticus 11.[15] Furthermore, there is no prohibition on marriage in the Torah. Rather, God commands us to be fruitful and multiply. Others have supposed it to mean that so long as unclean meats are eaten "with gratitude" and with prayer, the meat is sanctified by God's Word and rendered permissible. This, too, is a misunderstanding of the Apostle's words. Let's uncover the real doctrine of demons.

Gnosticism and Asceticism

There is no prohibition on marriage in the Torah. In fact, traditional Judaism regards marriage as obligatory. In Judaism, sexual relations within marriage are not only permissible, they are encouraged. Therefore, it is erroneous to suppose that the "doctrine of demons" Paul refers to in 1 Timothy 4 has anything to do with traditional Jewish teaching on marriage and food. On the other hand, the early Gnostics did teach abstinence from sex, marriage and certain foods.[16] What is Gnosticism? Gnosticism was a troublesome perversion of Judaism (and subsequently Christianity) with which the Apostles were forced to contend and refute. Among Gnosticism's many strange teachings, some adherents taught that the physical world was intrinsically evil, and that the human body was a cage for the spirit. Only by rejecting the physical world and its delights could the spirit be set free to soar. Gnostics taught the dualistic belief in which the spiritual world is regarded as good and the physical world is regarded as evil. Some branches of Gnosticism manifested in extreme asceticism. Their adherents swore off sex and marriage and often subjected themselves to long fasts and rigid diets in order to weaken their bodies so their spirits could be freed. They believed that the secret to setting the spirit free was the secret knowledge (*gnosis*) imparted by divine revelation, usually through visions or angelic encounters. It is the heresy of Gnosticism that Paul addresses in 1 Timothy and Colossians.

Everything Created by God is Good

In his first letter to Timothy, Paul uses Genesis 1:31 to refute the teachings of the Gnostics. Whereas they taught that certain foods were intrinsically bad because they were part of the physical world, Paul points out that the Torah says, "everything created by God is good," as it says, "God saw all that he had made, and it was very good." (Genesis 1:31) This goodness also applies to foods and to sexual relations, both of which were created to be enjoyed.

Paul does not, however, mean to imply that we are free to indulge in every and any food and every and any sexual relationship. Rather, he says that permissible sex and permissible foods are "sanctified by means of the word of God and prayer." Sanctified means set apart. That is to say, the Torah (God's Word) has "set apart" permissible foods (Leviticus 11) and permissible sexual relationships (Leviticus 18) by defining them as different from those that are not permissible. Marriage and eating food are both sanctified by God's commandments permitting certain forms of them, while forbidding other forms. In addition, according to Jewish tradition, marriage and food are both instituted with blessings, i.e., prayers of thanksgiving. This is why Paul says, "nothing is to be rejected if it is received with gratitude; for it is sanctified by means of the word of God and prayer." (1 Timothy 4:5)

We should not reject what God has created as good and has given to us to enjoy. But neither should we suppose that everything He has created is permissible. God's commandments say that intimacy with your neighbor's spouse is not permissible, nor is eating his dog.

Self-Made Religion

Paul labels Gnosticism—not the laws of clean and unclean—as a doctrine of demons. Similarly, he writes against Gnosticism in his letter to the Colossians. Colossi was not far from the province of Galatia, and the Colossian believers found themselves dealing with some of the same questions regarding Gentile circumcision (i.e., conversion) with which the Galatian communities struggled. In addition, the Colossians seem to have been incorporating Gnostic beliefs in their observances. Paul corrects this error in his letter to the Colossians:

> Let no one keep defrauding you of your prize by delighting in self-abasement and the worship of the angels, taking his stand on visions he has seen, inflated without cause by his fleshly mind ... If you have died with Messiah to the elementary principles of the world, why, as if you were living in the world, do you submit yourself to decrees, such as, "Do not handle, do not taste, do not touch!" (which all refer to things destined to perish with use)—in accordance with the commandments and teachings of men? These are matters which have, to be sure, the appearance of wisdom in self-made religion and self-abasement and

severe treatment of the body, but are of no value against fleshly indulgence. (Colossians 2:18–23)

Our traditional Christian interpretation of Colossians 2:20–21 suggests that Paul was calling the Torah's commands and prohibitions "the elementary principles of the world" and the "commandments and teachings of men." Because the beginning of the chapter refers to matters of Torah (Sabbaths, festivals, new moons, dietary laws [Colossians 2:16]), we assume that Paul is referring to those rites as "commands and teachings of men" all "destined to perish with use." This is wrong. "Elementary principles of the world" refers to paganism or Gnostic beliefs, not the commandments of God. Torah commands are teachings of God, not man. The larger context of the passage clarifies that Paul is referring to a Gnostic perversion of God's truth. It was apparently a supposed secret knowledge imparted by visions that advocated a high level of asceticism.

The religious tendencies Paul here describes are "self-made" and based upon the "commandments and teachings of men." They are "of no value against fleshly indulgence." The dietary laws of the Bible, on the other hand, are God-given and based on the commandments and teachings of God. Regarding those laws, Paul says, "All scripture is given by inspiration of God, and is profitable for doctrine, for reproof, for correction, for instruction in righteousness." (2 Timothy 3:16)

Shadows of Messiah

In Colossians 2, Paul defends the biblical laws saying, "Therefore no one is to act as your judge in regard to food or drink or in respect to a festival or a new moon or a Sabbath day—things which are a shadow of what is to come; and the substance belongs to Messiah." (Colossians 2:16–17) Regarding the biblical laws, Paul says that we should pay no heed to those who would judge us regarding our observance of them because they foreshadow things to come—a shadow cast by the substance of Messiah Himself. Every shadow has a shadow-caster, and Paul says that the biblical laws are like the shadow of Messiah. They show the shape of Messiah. They are God's laws and the substance of them belongs to Messiah.

Therefore, we may be certain that Paul is not speaking against the dietary laws in Colossians 2, but against a perverse religious system of asceticism that misapplies some observance of Torah. In Paul's view, the Gnostic worldview that denigrates the physical world is at variance with the Bible. The Bible declares, "And God saw all that He had made, and behold, it was very good." (Genesis 1:32)

Man Alive!
A Look Back at Church History

The New Testament, like any piece of literature, is context-dependent. When we read it outside of its context, it is impossible to accurately interpret its original meaning. Unfortunately for us, shortly after the age of the Apostles came to a close, there was a great schism between believing Gentiles and unbelieving Jews.

The political upheaval of the first and second Jewish revolts, coupled with Roman, state-sponsored persecution, forced non-Jewish believers to disassociate themselves from Judaism. At the same time, believers began to experience concentrated persecution within the synagogues and were actually expelled from participation in the Jewish congregation. As a result, many non-Jewish believers in Jesus were left trying to interpret the Bible with only a superficial knowledge of the original matrix from which it had come. The details of arguments over conversion, ritual purity, contact with non-Jews, contact with idols, and the minutia wrapped up in those arguments were all lost to us. We began to read the New Testament with a decidedly anti-Jewish posture, and interpreted the arguments of the Apostolic Communities as if they were anti-Jewish and anti-Torah arguments.

We quickly forgot that Jesus, the Apostles and all the early believers were Jewish and/or worshipping in a Jewish context. In the early second century, there was a popular uprising within Christianity with the aim of completely removing the Hebrew Scriptures (and most of the New Testament as well) in an attempt for total disassociation from Judaism.[17] Our early Christian faith took its traditional shape by defining itself in antithesis to Judaism. Therefore, we began to consider it praiseworthy and meritorious to violate God's dietary laws and the other laws that seemed conspicuously Jewish. Within a few centuries, we had begun to consider it a service to God to persecute and even torture and kill the Jewish people.

In today's world, the horror of the Nazi holocaust has shocked us to our senses. We are digging deeper into Bibles, digging deeper into Church history, and digging deeper into Jewish sources as we ask ourselves, "How could we have let this happen?" The result of this digging has yielded some real surprises. Like archaeologists digging through layers of rubble to find the foundations of the original city, we have begun to clear away years of misinterpretation and anti-Semitic theology. It is exciting work. One of the ancient treasures we have unearthed in this theological, archaeological dig is the biblical dietary laws. The really surprising thing is to realize that these laws might have actual, practical application for us today.

In the final analysis, whether or not one decides to observe the biblical dietary laws is certainly a personal decision. But let's not remove the New Testament from its historical context in order to justify our decision.

Endnotes

[1] Matthew 8:4, Mark 1:44, Luke 5:14
[2] Deuteronomy 17:20
[3] According to the Bible, some "unclean" states cannot be transmitted; other "unclean states" can be. The term "ritually contaminating" refers to the latter state, whereby a person's "uncleanness" can be passed on to other people.
[4] Numbers 19:22
[5] For details of how food might be construed to be made unclean and defiling, see Tim Hegg's 2002 article "Did God Change His Mind About Food?" at torahresource.com.
[6] Exodus 34:15
[7] For example, see Leviticus 19:34.
[8] Exodus 34:15
[9] Revelation 2:14, 20
[10] 1 Corinthians 10:23
[11] 1 Corinthians 8:9–13
[12] 1 Corinthians 10:27–28
[13] 1 Corinthians 5:11
[14] Ephesians 5:5–7

[15] Acts 21:24, Acts 23:1, Acts 25:8, Acts 28:17, 1 Corinthians 9:21

[16] Such aestheticism also characterized the Ebionites, an early splinter of the Jesus movement.

[17] Marcion's heresy.

Appendices

Bible and Apocrypha Passages

List of Clean and Unclean Animals

Resources

Bibliography

Scripture Reference Index

Subject Index

Bible and Apocrypha Passages

Leviticus 11

1 The LORD spoke again to Moses and to Aaron, saying to them,
2 "Speak to the sons of Israel, saying, 'These are the creatures which you may eat from all the animals that are on the earth.
3 'Whatever divides a hoof, thus making split hoofs, and chews the cud, among the animals, that you may eat.
4 'Nevertheless, you are not to eat of these, among those which chew the cud, or among those which divide the hoof: the camel, for though it chews cud, it does not divide the hoof, it is unclean to you.
5 'Likewise, the shaphan, for though it chews cud, it does not divide the hoof, it is unclean to you;
6 the rabbit also, for though it chews cud, it does not divide the hoof, it is unclean to you;
7 and the pig, for though it divides the hoof, thus making a split hoof, it does not chew cud, it is unclean to you.
8 'You shall not eat of their flesh nor touch their carcasses; they are unclean to you.
9 'These you may eat, whatever is in the water: all that have fins and scales, those in the water, in the seas or in the rivers, you may eat.
10 'But whatever is in the seas and in the rivers that does not have fins and scales among all the teeming life of the water, and among all the living creatures that are in the water, they are detestable things to you,
11 and they shall be abhorrent to you; you may not eat of their flesh, and their carcasses you shall detest.
12 'Whatever in the water does not have fins and scales is abhorrent to you.
13 'These, moreover, you shall detest among the birds; they are abhorrent, not to be eaten: the eagle and the vulture and the buzzard,
14 and the kite and the falcon in its kind,
15 every raven in its kind,

16 and the ostrich and the owl and the sea gull and the hawk in its kind,
17 and the little owl and the cormorant and the great owl,
18 and the white owl and the pelican and the carrion vulture,
19 and the stork, the heron in its kinds, and the hoopoe, and the bat.
20 'All the winged insects that walk on all fours are detestable to you.
21 'Yet these you may eat among all the winged insects which walk on all fours: those which have above their feet jointed legs with which to jump on the earth.
22 'These of them you may eat: the locust in its kinds, and the devastating locust in its kinds, and the cricket in its kinds, and the grasshopper in its kinds.
23 'But all other winged insects which are four-footed are detestable to you.
24 'By these, moreover, you will be made unclean: whoever touches their carcasses becomes unclean until evening,
25 and whoever picks up any of their carcasses shall wash his clothes and be unclean until evening.
26 'Concerning all the animals which divide the hoof but do not make a split hoof, or which do not chew cud, they are unclean to you: whoever touches them becomes unclean.
27 'Also whatever walks on its paws, among all the creatures that walk on all fours, are unclean to you; whoever touches their carcasses becomes unclean until evening,
28 and the one who picks up their carcasses shall wash his clothes and be unclean until evening; they are unclean to you.
29 'Now these are to you the unclean among the swarming things which swarm on the earth: the mole, and the mouse, and the great lizard in its kinds,
30 and the gecko, and the crocodile, and the lizard, and the sand reptile, and the chameleon.
31 'These are to you the unclean among all the swarming things; whoever touches them when they are dead becomes unclean until evening.
32 'Also anything on which one of them may fall when they are dead becomes unclean, including any wooden article, or clothing, or a skin, or a sack—any article of which use is made—it shall be put in the water and be unclean until evening, then it becomes clean.
33 'As for any earthenware vessel into which one of them may fall, whatever is in it becomes unclean and you shall break the vessel.

34 'Any of the food which may be eaten, on which water comes, shall become unclean, and any liquid which may be drunk in every vessel shall become unclean.

35 'Everything, moreover, on which part of their carcass may fall becomes unclean; an oven or a stove shall be smashed; they are unclean and shall continue as unclean to you.

36 'Nevertheless a spring or a cistern collecting water shall be clean, though the one who touches their carcass shall be unclean.

37 'If a part of their carcass falls on any seed for sowing which is to be sown, it is clean.

38 'Though if water is put on the seed and a part of their carcass falls on it, it is unclean to you.

39 'Also if one of the animals dies which you have for food, the one who touches its carcass becomes unclean until evening.

40 'He too, who eats some of its carcass shall wash his clothes and be unclean until evening, and the one who picks up its carcass shall wash his clothes and be unclean until evening.

41 'Now every swarming thing that swarms on the earth is detestable, not to be eaten.

42 'Whatever crawls on its belly, and whatever walks on all fours, whatever has many feet, in respect to every swarming thing that swarms on the earth, you shall not eat them, for they are detestable.

43 'Do not render yourselves detestable through any of the swarming things that swarm; and you shall not make yourselves unclean with them so that you become unclean.

44 'For I am the LORD your God. Consecrate yourselves therefore, and be holy, for I am holy. And you shall not make yourselves unclean with any of the swarming things that swarm on the earth.

45 'For I am the LORD who brought you up from the land of Egypt to be your God; thus you shall be holy, for I am holy.'"

46 This is the law regarding the animal and the bird, and every living thing that moves in the waters and everything that swarms on the earth,

47 to make a distinction between the unclean and the clean, and between the edible creature and the creature which is not to be eaten.

Leviticus 11 *New American Standard Bible*

Mark 7:1–23

1 The Pharisees and some of the scribes gathered around Him when they had come from Jerusalem,
2 and had seen that some of His disciples were eating their bread with impure hands, that is, unwashed.
3 (For the Pharisees and all the Jews do not eat unless they carefully wash their hands, thus observing the traditions of the elders;
4 and when they come from the market place, they do not eat unless they cleanse themselves; and there are many other things which they have received in order to observe, such as the washing of cups and pitchers and copper pots.)
5 The Pharisees and the scribes asked Him, "Why do Your disciples not walk according to the tradition of the elders, but eat their bread with impure hands?"
6 And He said to them, "Rightly did Isaiah prophesy of you hypocrites, as it is written: 'THIS PEOPLE HONORS ME WITH THEIR LIPS, BUT THEIR HEART IS FAR AWAY FROM ME.
7 'BUT IN VAIN DO THEY WORSHIP ME, TEACHING AS DOCTRINES THE PRECEPTS OF MEN.'
8 "Neglecting the commandment of God, you hold to the tradition of men."
9 He was also saying to them, "You are experts at setting aside the commandment of God in order to keep your tradition.
10 "For Moses said, 'HONOR YOUR FATHER AND YOUR MOTHER'; and, 'HE WHO SPEAKS EVIL OF FATHER OR MOTHER, IS TO BE PUT TO DEATH';
11 but you say, 'If a man says to his father or his mother, whatever I have that would help you is Corban (that is to say, given to God),'
12 you no longer permit him to do anything for his father or his mother;
13 thus invalidating the word of God by your tradition which you have handed down; and you do many things such as that."
14 After He called the crowd to Him again, He began saying to them, "Listen to Me, all of you, and understand:
15 there is nothing outside the man which can defile him if it goes into him; but the things which proceed out of the man are what defile the man.
16 ["If anyone has ears to hear, let him hear."]
17 When he had left the crowd and entered the house, His disciples questioned Him about the parable.

18 And He said to them, "Are you so lacking in understanding also? Do you not understand that whatever goes into the man from outside cannot defile him,

19 because it does not go into his heart, but into his stomach, and is eliminated?" (Thus He declared all foods clean.)

20 And He was saying, "That which proceeds out of the man, that is what defiles the man.

21 "For from within, out of the heart of men, proceed the evil thoughts, fornications, thefts, murders, adulteries,

22 deeds of coveting and wickedness, as well as deceit, sensuality, envy, slander, pride and foolishness.

23 "All these evil things proceed from within and defile the man."

Mark 7:1–23 *New American Standard Bible*

2 Maccabees 6:18–31

18 Eleazar, one of the scribes in high position, a man now advanced in age and of noble presence, was being forced to open his mouth to eat swine's flesh.

19 But he, welcoming death with honor rather than life with pollution, went up to the the rack of his own accord, spitting out the flesh,

20 as men ought to go who have the courage to refuse things that it is not right to taste, even for the natural love of life.

21 Those who were in charge of that unlawful sacrifice took the man aside because of their long acquaintance with him, and privately urged him to bring meat of his own providing, proper for him to use, and pretend that he was eating the flesh of the sacrificial meal which had been commanded by the king,

22 so that by doing this he might be saved from death, and be treated kindly on account of his old friendship with them.

23 But making a high resolve, worthy of his years and the dignity of his old age and the gray hairs which he had reached with distinction and his excellent life even from childhood, and moreover according to the holy God-given law, he declared himself quickly, telling them to send him to Hades.

24 "Such pretense is not worthy of our time of life," he said, "lest many of the young should suppose that Eleazar in his ninetieth year has gone over to an alien religion,

25 and through my pretense, for the sake of living a brief moment longer, they should be led astray because of me, while I defile and disgrace my old age.

26 For even if for the present I should avoid the punishment of men, yet whether I live or die I shall not escape the hands of the Almighty.

27 Therefore, by manfully giving up my life now, I will show myself worthy of my old age

28 and leave to the young a noble example of how to die a good death willingly and nobly for the revered and holy laws." When he had said this, he went at once to the rack.

29 And those who a little before had acted toward him with good will now changed to ill will, because the words he had uttered were in their opinion sheer madness.

30 When he was about to die under the blows, he groaned aloud and said: "It is clear to the Lord in his holy knowledge that, though I might have been saved from death, I am enduring terrible sufferings in my body under this beating, but in my soul I am glad to suffer these things because I fear him."

31 So in this way he died, leaving in his death an example of nobility and a memorial of courage, not only to the young but to the great body of his nation.

---

2 Maccabees 6:18–31 *Revised Standard Version*

List of Clean and Unclean Animals

Clean Animals

The characteristics of clean and unclean animals are clearly spelled out in Leviticus 11. While some animals are specifically mentioned there, the following list is mostly based on man's interpretation of those characteristics. As such, other clean and unclean animal lists may vary.

Animals that Chew the Cud and Part the Hoof

- Antelope
- Bison (buffalo)
- Caribou
- Cattle (beef, veal)
- Deer (venison)
- Elk
- Gazelle
- Giraffe
- Goat
- Hart
- Ibex
- Moose
- Ox
- Reindeer
- Sheep (lamb, mutton)

Fish with Fins and Scales

- Anchovy
- Barracuda
- Bass
- Black pomfret (or monchong)
- Bluefish
- Bluegill
- Carp
- Cod
- Crappie
- Drum
- Flounder
- Grouper
- Grunt
- Haddock
- Hake
- Halibut

Hardhead

Herring (or alewife)

Kingfish

Mackerel (or cobia)

Mahi-mahi (or dorado, dolphinfish [not to be confused with the mammal dolphin])

Minnow

Mullet

Perch (or bream)

Pike (or pickerel or jack)

Pollack (or pollock or Boston bluefish)

Rockfish

Salmon

Sardine (or pilchard)

Shad

Silver hake (or whiting)

Smelt (or frost fish or ice fish)

Snapper (or ebu, jobfish, lehi, onaga, opakapaka or uku)

Sole

Steelhead

Sucker

Sunfish

Tarpon

Trout (or weakfish)

Tuna (or ahi, aku, albacore, bonito or tombo)

Turbot (except European turbot)

Whitefish

Birds with Clean Characteristics

Chicken

Dove

Duck

Goose

Grouse

Guinea fowl

Partridge

Peafowl

Pheasant

Pigeon

Prairie chicken

Ptarmigan

Quail

Sagehen

Sparrow (and other songbirds)

Swan

Teal

Turkey

Insects

Types of locusts that may include crickets and grasshoppers

Unclean Animals

Animals with Unclean Characteristics

Swine
- Boar
- Peccary
- Pig (hog, bacon, ham, lard, pork, most sausage and pepperoni)

Canines
- Coyote
- Dog
- Fox
- Hyena
- Jackal
- Wolf

Felines
- Cat
- Cheetah
- Leopard
- Lion
- Panther
- Tiger

Equines
- Ass
- Donkey
- Horse
- Mule
- Onager
- Zebra (quagga)

Other
- Armadillo
- Badger
- Bear
- Beaver
- Camel
- Elephant
- Gorilla
- Groundhog
- Hare
- Hippopotamus
- Kangaroo
- Llama (alpaca, vicuña)
- Mole
- Monkey
- Mouse
- Muskrat
- Opossum
- Porcupine
- Rabbit
- Raccoon
- Rat
- Rhinoceros
- Skunk
- Slug
- Snail (escargot)
- Squirrel
- Wallaby
- Weasel
- Wolverine
- Worm
- All insects except some in the locust family

Marine Animals Without Scales and Fins

Fish
- Bullhead
- Catfish
- Eel
- European turbot
- Marlin
- Paddlefish
- Shark
- Stickleback
- Squid
- Sturgeon (includes most caviar)
- Swordfish

Shellfish
- Abalone
- Clam
- Crab
- Crayfish
- Lobster
- Mussel
- Prawn
- Oyster
- Scallop
- Shrimp

Soft body
- Cuttlefish
- Jellyfish
- Limpet
- Octopus
- Squid (calamari)

Sea mammals
- Dolphin
- Otter
- Porpoise
- Seal
- Walrus
- Whale

Birds of Prey, Scavengers and Others
- Albatross
- Bat
- Bittern
- Buzzard
- Condor
- Coot
- Cormorant
- Crane
- Crow
- Cuckoo
- Eagle
- Flamingo
- Grebe
- Grosbeak
- Gull
- Hawk
- Heron
- Kite
- Lapwing
- Loon
- Magpie
- Osprey
- Ostrich
- Owl
- Parrot

Pelican
Penguin
Plover
Rail
Raven
Roadrunner
Sandpiper
Seagull
Stork
Swallow
Swift
Vulture
Water hen
Woodpecker

Reptiles
Alligator
Caiman
Crocodile
Lizard
Snake
Turtle

Amphibians
Blindworm
Frog
Newt
Salamander
Toad

Reprinted by permission of United Church of God, an International Association, "What Does the Bible Teach about Clean and Unclean Meats?" *www.ucg.org/booklets/CU*.

Resources

Given how difficult it is to find meat products that attempt to both raise and slaughter cattle according to God's design, I am encouraged that there are a few resources that meet this need. And, although they are not cheap, if you adhere to the "special occasions" meat-eating guideline, you might actually be able to reduce your meat spending while increasing the quality of the food you eat.

▪ Beyond Organic

www.livebeyondorganic.com

Founder Jordan Rubin is a Jewish believer who is passionate about providing consumers high quality, biblically raised and slaughtered organic beef. Although it is not *kosher* certified, this company uses *kosher* kill methods and state-of-the-art *kosher* equipment in order to properly drain the blood. In addition, they never stun their cattle, which some *kosher* plants do post slaughter. Finally, they remove the prohibited fat surrounding the kidneys (and do not use it in their ground beef or hot dogs).

Because I feel like their products are most in line with what I believe God's design is (for ground beef and hot dogs), and the best way to "eat biblically" in how the animals are treated in life and in death, I am exploring this avenue for high quality beef.

More information about their products is available on their website, or visit mine at http://holycowhope.mybeyondorganic.com. Although they use a non-traditional distribution method (network marketing), I plan to pursue it given that their vision and values overlap so closely with mine.

Kol Foods
www.kolfoods.com

Their beef is 100% grass fed and certified kosher. Although it is quite pricey, they do have buyers clubs in several big cities. They also sell lamb, chicken and turkey.

EcoGlatt
www.ecoglatt.com

Temple Grandin raved about this small plant and its slaughter methods, as well as how the animals are raised and fed. Their website currently does not say how to actually buy this meat.

Wise Organic Pastures
www.wiseorganicpastures.com

This small organic kosher company sells wholesome, organic kosher meat. Although their website lists beef, at the time of this writing they only have poultry.

Other Resources

Feel free to friend me on Facebook or visit my two Facebook pages: "Biblical Eating Resources" and "Holy Cow by Hope Egan."

Bibliography

Booker, Bruce, Ph.D. *A Call to Holiness*, 1994.

Brown, Michael L. *Answering Jewish Objections to Jesus*. Baker Books, 2000.

Colbert, Don, M.D. *What Would Jesus Eat?* Thomas Nelson, Inc., 2002.

Eidlitz, Rabbi E. *Is it Kosher? Encyclopedia of Kosher Foods, Facts & Fallacies*. Feldheim Publishers Ltd., 1992.

Fallon, Sally. *Nourishing Traditions: The Cookbook that Challenges Politically Correct Nutrition and the Diet Dictocrats*. New Trend Publishing, 2001.

First Fruits of Zion. *HaYesod*. First Fruits of Zion, 1999.

Friedman, David, Ph.D. *They Loved Torah: What Yeshua's First Followers Really Thought about the Law*. Lederer Books, 2001.

Frydland, Rachmiel. *What the Rabbis Know about the Messiah*. Messianic Publishing Company, 2002.

Grandin, Temple and Regenstein, Joe. "Religious slaughter and animal welfare: a discussion for meat scientists" Pages 72–73 in Meat Focus International, March 1994, published by CAB International.

Hegg, Tim. *Introduction to Torah Living*. TorahResource.com, 2002.

Hegg, Tim. *It is Often Said Volumes 1 & 2*. First Fruits of Zion, 2003.

Hegg, Tim. *The Letter Writer*. First Fruits of Zion, 2002.

Jacobson, Michael D. *The World on Health: A Biblical and Medical Overview of How to Care for Your Body and Mind*. Moody Press, 2000.

Josephson, Elmer A. *God's Key to Health and Happiness*. Revell, 1976.

Kaiser, Walter & Silva, Moises. *An Introduction to Biblical Hermeneutics*. Zondervan, 1994.

Kaiser, Walter C. *Messiah in the Old Testament*. Zondervan, 1995.

Keil & Delitzsch. *Commentary on the Old Testament*. Freeware via *www.e-sword.net*.

Kantzer, Kenneth. *Life Application Study Bible*. Tyndale House Publishers, 2000.

Lancaster, D.T. *Torah Club Volume Five*. First Fruits of Zion, 2004.

Lerner, Ben. *Body By God*. Thomas Nelson, 2003.

Lubavitch Women's Cookbook Publications. *Body & Soul: A Handbook for Kosher Living*. 1989.

Lyman, Howard F. *Mad Cowboy: Plain Truth from the Cattle Rancher Who Won't Eat Meat*. Scribner, 2001.

Mathison, Keith A. *Dispensationalism: Rightly Dividing the People of God?* Presbyterian and Reformed Publishing Company, 1995.

McMillen, S.I. and Stern, David E. *None of These Diseases: The Bible's Health Secrets for the 21st Century*. Fleming H. Revell, 2000.

Moskala, Jiri. *The Laws of Clean & Unclean Animals in Leviticus 11: Their Nature, Theology & Rationale*. Adventists Theological Society Publications, 2000.

Murti, Vasu. *They Shall Not Hurt or Destroy: Animal Rights and Vegetarianism in the Western Religious Traditions*. Vegetarian Advocates Press, 2003.

Regenstein, J.M. et al. "The Kosher and Halal Food Laws." Pages 111–127 in *Comprehensive Reviews in Food Science and Food Safety*, vol. 2, 2003.

Robbins, John. *Diet for a New America*. Stillpoint Publishing, 1987.

Rosenberg, Avrohom Yosif. *Mishnah Kodashim Vol. II(a): Chullin*. Mesorah Publications, 2003.

Rubenstein, Shmuel. *The Kashrus Manual: A Compendium of Laws and Customs*. University of Toronto Press Incorporated, 2000.

Rubin, Barry. *You Bring the Bagels, I'll Bring the Gospel*. Lederer Books, 1997.

Rubin, Jordan, N.M.D., Ph.D. *The Maker's Diet*. Siloam, 2004.

Russell, Rex, M.D. *What the Bible Says about Healthy Living*. Regal, 1996.

Slifkin, Rabbi Nosson. *The Camel, the Hare & the Hyrax: A study of the laws of animals with one kosher sign in light of modern zoology*. Targum Press, 2004.

Stern, David H. *The Jewish New Testament Commentary*. Jewish New Testament Publications, 1996.

Schwartz, Richard H, Ph.D. *Judaism and Vegetarianism*. Lantern Books, 2001.

Tessler, Gordon. *The Genesis Diet*. Be Well Publications, 1996.

Yancey, Philip & Brand, Paul, Dr. *Fearfully and Wonderfully Made*. Zondervan, 1980.

Yeager, Selene, et al. *The Doctors Book of Food Remedies*. Rodale, 1998.

Scripture Reference Index

Genesis

1	23
1:29	12–13, 15, 25,
1:29	30–32, 39, 66, 80, 84
1:31	124
1:32	127
2:9	13
2:16–17	15
6:3	90
6:9	14
7	23
7:2	14, 15, 25
8:20	15
9	23
9:1	14
9:3	14–15, 26
18	16
18:1–3, 7–8	81
32:32	67

Exodus

12	5
12:37–38	16, 20
20:2	19
20:10	71
21:28–29	79
23:5	71
23:19	77, 78
34:12–15	55
34:15	117
34:26	77

Leviticus

3:17	61
7:23, 25	65
11	3, 5, 8, 14, 20–25, 30–32, 34, 39, 40, 49, 53, 54, 56, 57, 63, 64, 83, 85, 89, 97, 98, 100, 103, 107, 112, 123, 125
11:3–8	22
11:3, 9	22–23
11:4	23
11:9–12	22–23
11:13–19	22
11:20–23	23
11:33–36	52
11:44, 45	24
11:46–47	22
11:47	106
12:2	99
15:25	99
17:11	61
18	125
19	21
19:3–11	21
22:8	72

Numbers

15:15–16	20
19:11	19

Deuteronomy

4	43
4:6–7	43
4:40	19
6	5
12:15–16	66

12:20 25
12:32 39
13:4–5 104
4 . . . . 25, 30
14:3 23
14:3–20 20
14:21 77
18:10–12 23
22:4 71
22:6–7 71
23:12–13 19

Ezra
7:10 41

Psalms
24:1 119
104:14, 21, 25, 27–28 11
119:34 18
119:47 18
119:97 18
119:127 18

Proverbs
6:26 105

Isaiah
66:16–17 57

Ezekiel
4:11–15 110
4:13 105
4:14 110
18:4 18
36:26–27 18

Daniel
1:15 13

Zechariah
12 92

Malachi
3:6–7 43
3:7 44
4:4–5 44

Matthew
3:4 35
5:17 . . . . 49, 52
5:17–19 . . . . 50, 51, 58
6:25 11
8:3 99
23:2–3 78
23:4 . . . . 42, 50

Mark
1:6 35
1:41 99
7 . . . . 52, 53, 103
7:1–23 . . . . 52, 58, 103–108
7:3 52
7:7 53
7:8 53
7:9 53
7:13 53
7:14–23 53
7:17–18 107
7:19 . . . . 103, 107–108

Luke
7:14 99

John
10:22 45
18:28 111

Acts
10 . . . . 54, 109, 110, 117
10:13 109
10:14 . . . . 54, 112
10:14–15 54
10:17 . . . . 54, 113
10:19 54
10:19–20 113
10:28 . . . . 55, 111, 112
10:28–29 111
10:34 55
11:1–18 111
11:5–18 55
15 . . . . 61, 72
15:20 118

15:29. . . . . 55, 72

Romans

5 51
6 51
6:15. 50–52
6:23. 18
7:12. 50
8:2. 50
10:4. 51, 52
14 . . . . 115, 117, 121
14:2, 5. 7
14:2–4. 120
14:14. . . . . 115, 120
14:20–21 121

1 Corinthians

8–10 . . . . 55, 115, 121
8:8. 120
10:14. 119
10:20–21 119
10:25. . . . . 7, 55
10:25–26 119
10:30–31 119

Galatians

2:10–15. 115
2:11–13. 55
2:11–14. 116
2:11–15. 111

Ephesians

2:8 7

Colossians

2 . . . . 126, 127
2:16–17. 126
2:18–23. . . . . 123, 126
2:20–21. 126

1 Thessalonians

4:3. 42
5:23–24. 87

1 Timothy

4 124
4:1–5. 123
4:4 56
4:4–5. 7
4:5 125

2 Timothy

3:16. 126

Hebrews

10:4. 100

1 Peter

1:14–16. 24

Revelation

12:17. 57

Subject Index

A

Abraham, 15, 81
Adam, 14, 15, 17, 25
adhesions, 68
akathartos, 118, 121
antibiotics, 35, 36, 69, 74, 84
Apocrypha, 47, 135
assimilation, 111, 116

B

bacon, 63, 143
Barnabas, 116
Beyond Organic, xiii, 147
Biblically Kosher, vii, 89, 90, 91
birds, 22, 33, 34, 35, 142, 144
blood, 31
  and Acts 15, 72
  and Science, 62
  avoiding, 61, 63, 67
  avoiding excess, 67
  chemistry, 33
  draining, 66, 67
  eating, 61
  life is in the, 61
  pressure, 34
  prohibition against eating, 67
  pudding, 63
  sausage, 63
  to pour it out, 66
blood and fat, 72
bodek, 68
buzzards, 22

C

captive bolt, 70
carbon dioxide, 30, 70
carcasses, 100, 135, 136
chew the cud, 22, 31, 32, 135
chicken, 63
child sacrifice, 23, 41
cholera, 33
Church History, 129
circumcision, 125
Colbert, Don, xi, 31, 39
common, 111, 112, 117, 118, 120, 121
contaminating, 104, 106, 111
Cornelius, 55, 112, 113, 116

D

daily, 5, 85
David, 17, 18
detestable, 23, 57, 135, 136, 137
dishes, 3, 7, 77, 78
  separating, 78
  two sets, 3, 77
Dispensational theology, 56
doctrines of demons, 56, 123
duck, 23, 35, 142

E

Eby, Aaron, vii, 89, 90
Eleazar, 44, 139
Elijah, 44, 47
Elizabeth, 3, 4, 5, 7, 77
exile, 41, 43
Exodus, 16, 27, 40

Ezekiel, 110
Ezra, 41

F

factory farms, 69
farmers, 31, 33, 36, 68
fat, 61, 64, 65, 67, 72, 74
  and kosher meat, 65
  avoiding, 61, 65
  belongs to the Lord, 65
  hog, 64
  plant-based, 65
fellowship
  table-fellowship with Jews, 111, 117
  with Gentiles, 116
fences around the Torah, 42, 43, 52, 53, 77, 79, 111, 116
fins and scales, 22, 23, 33, 34, 135, 141
First Fruits of Zion, vii, 7, 89, 90
fish, 13, 22, 33, 34, 36, 141, 144
flocks, 15, 42
food
  "polluted by idols", 117
  sacrificed to idols, 119
future is invading the present, 56

G

The Genesis Diet, 6, 38, 150
Gentiles
  and circumcision, 125
  and food sacrificed to idols, 119
  and Peter's vision, 113
  and table-fellowship with Jews, 111
  and uncleanness, 111
  classified as unclean, 111
  contact with, 121
  dwelling places of, 111
  eating with, 110, 111, 116
  entering the homes of, 111
  food prepared by, 117
  not to associate with, 111
  prohibition on eating with, 115
  separation between Jews and Gentiles, 116
Gnosticism, 124, 125
Gnostics
  dualistic belief, 124
  taught abstinence, 124
  taught abstinence from certain foods, 56
goats, 16, 22, 38, 65, 77, 79, 98
goose, 35, 142
Temple Grandin, 64, 67, 74, 75
grasshoppers, 23, 35, 142
Great Assembly, 41
Greeks, 44, 45

H

ham, 4, 52, 63, 105, 108
hand washing, 52, 53, 104
Hanukkah, 45
Heart of Wisdom, 10, 89, 90
Hegg, Tim, vii
Hellenize, 44
herbivores, 31, 32, 36, 38
herds, 15
history
  Church, 129
  Israel's, 40
holocaust, 130
hormones, 36, 69, 71, 74
humane treatment, 70, 75

I

idolatry
  contact with, 119
idols, 117, 118, 120, 129
  contact with, 129
  don't worship, 21
  food sacrificed to, 118, 119, 121
  meat sacrificed to, 55, 117, 120
immersion in water, 101
insects, 23, 33, 35, 136, 142, 143

J

Jacob, 16, 54, 74
James, 17, 116
Jerusalem Council, 61
Jesus
  "declared all foods clean", 103
  "fulfilled the Law", 5, 7, 49, 50
  blood of, 62
  what would Jesus eat?, 39
Jews and non-Jews
  barrier between, 42
  God's laws applied to both, 20
  God's people included both, 59
  in fellowship together, 54
  on equal ground, 55
  Torah given to both, 20
  unbliblical separation
      between, 43
Johns Hopkins, 33
John the Baptist, 23, 35, 47
Joshua, 17

K

koinos, 118, 120, 121
kosher
  benefits, 67
  certification, 68, 70
  certified, 69
  practices, 67
  slaughtering, 64, 66
  standards, 66
  three main aspects of, 63
  what is, 63
Ku Klux Klan, xv

L

Lancaster, D. Thomas, vii, xii,
    52, 54, 55, 62, 79, 84, 86,
    89, 90, 91, 95, 101
lard, 64, 143
Law
  "will go forth from Zion", 73
  Jesus fulfilled, 5
  Jesus not setting aside, 108
  Messiah fulfilled, 49
  not to depart from, 103, 108
  of Moses, 50, 51
law
  dietary, 118
  forbidding food sacrificed to
      idols, 117
  fulfilled, 50, 84, 85
  jewish, 70
legalism, 50, 51
lifespan, 36
locusts, 23, 35, 36, 142
loving God, 86
loving our neighbor, 86
Luther, xv

M

Maccabee, 45
Maccabees, 47, 139
Mad Cow Disease, 31
mammals, 22, 31, 33, 144
marriage, 9, 11, 29, 30, 37, 123,
    124, 125
meat
  after the time of Noah, 15
  certified organic, 72
  food laws, 16
  market, 7, 55, 119
  organic, 68, 72
  packers/distributors, 68, 69, 70
  producers/farmers, 68
  red, 13
  sacrificed to idols, 117, 119,
      120
  unclean, 23
meat and dairy, 3, 4, 64, 77, 80,
    91
mercury, 34
Messiah, xv, 7, 8, 18, 20
  "is the end of the Law", 49, 51
  fulfilled the Law, 49
  in the Hebrew Scriptures, 26
  meaning of the word, xvi
  Torah leads us to, 17
  Torah reveals aspects of, 17
milk

and digestion of meat, 80
and honey, 65
and meat, 77, 78
cooking meat in, 79
goat, 79
Mishnah, 42, 67, 104, 111
mixed multitude, 16, 20, 40
Moses, 51, 66, 74, 78, 104, 111
  "remember the Law of", 44
  Five Books of, 16
  law of, 50
Murti, 87

N

Noah, 4, 13, 14, 15, 17, 25, 61, 83
nomos, 50
non-Jews
  contact with, 129
  mixed multitude, 40

O

omnivores, 31, 32, 36
Oral Law, 42
Oral Torah, 42, 43, 54, 104, 105
organic, 68, 69, 72, 73, 74
organ meat, 65
Orthodox Judaism, 8, 117
oysters, 22, 33

P

pareve, 80
Passover, 5, 8, 17, 35, 36, 42, 47
Paul, 123
  "nothing is unclean", 120
  addresses Gnostic heresy, 124, 126
  and eating meat sacrificed to idols, 117, 119
  and his confrontation with Peter, 116
  and the dietary laws, 115
  defends biblical laws, 126
  observed the Torah, 123
Pentateuch, 16

Peter's dream, 54, 109
Peter's vision, 109, 110, 115, 116
pigs, 15, 22, 25, 31, 32, 33, 36
pork, 30, 33, 44, 63, 83, 84, 85
producers, 35, 68, 84
prophecy, 44, 47

Q

quail, 35, 142

R

Reformation, xv
remedy, 101
rendering, 74
ribs, 4, 6, 40, 63, 85
ritual purity, 97, 106, 107, 129
Rubin, Jordan, xi, 147
ruminants, 22, 27, 32
Russell, Rex, xi, 12, 32, 34, 80

S

Sages, 41, 43, 53, 64, 74, 79, 82
Salmon, 22, 34, 142
salting and soaking, 67
salvation, 19, 20, 37, 83, 99, 100
Sampson, Robin, 90
sausage, 63, 143
  casing, 63
scavenger, 25, 35, 63
Schwartz, 87
seder, 42, 47
shadow of what is to come, 126
shechitah, 66, 71, 72
shellfish, xi, 3, 6, 9, 83, 84, 85, 113, 144
shochet, 66, 67, 68
shrimp, xi, 5, 22, 40, 144
Sinai, 14, 16, 40, 44, 104
slaughter, 64, 66, 67, 68, 70, 71, 73, 75
slaughtering, 64, 67, 72, 74
  humane, 70
  kosher, 66
  methods, 70
  technique, 64

Slifkin, Nosson, 27, 150
Spanish Inquisition, xv
split hoof, 22, 135, 136
Spurlock, Rick, vii
steroids, 68
strangled, 61, 72
strangulation, 72
stunning, 70
stunning method
  carbon dioxide poisoning, 70
  electric, 70
  single captive bolt, 70

T

Tabernacle, 65, 84, 97, 98, 100
table-fellowship, 111, 117
Talmud, 78, 105
Temple, 21, 44, 45, 58
Temple sacrifices, 58, 62, 66
Tessler, Gordon, xi, 6
Torah
  Jesus lived out, 17
  purposes of, 17
  the Hebrew word, 17
  to whom given?, 20
  what is, 16
torn, 68, 72, 110
tradition, 106, 113, 118
  and the commandments of God, 107

Jewish, 78
of men, 106
of the elders, 105, 106
Pharisaic, 104, 105
traditions, 3, 14, 42, 43, 52, 53, 78, 80, 90, 91, 111, 116
turkey, 23, 35, 142
turkey bacon, 57

U

unclean heart, 106, 107
unclean meat, 44, 45, 84, 103, 108, 110, 121, 123
under law, 5, 49, 50, 51
University of Illinois, 5
unwashed hands, 52, 104, 106
USDA, 65, 68, 70, 71, 74

V

vegetables, 7, 12, 13, 80, 84, 86, 117, 120
vegetarian, 3, 13, 32, 36, 83, 90
Vegetarianism, 13, 26, 31, 83
vegetarian animals, 32, 63
vultures, 22, 25, 63

W

What the Bible Says about Healthy Living Cookbook, 89

Best selling author Hope Egan has written a variety of books, including *Holy Cow! Does God Care about What We Eat?* and the *What the Bible Says about Healthy Living Cookbook: Simple and Tasty Recipes Featuring God's Ingredients*. She has also written for numerous magazines and websites, including *Faith and Fitness Magazine* and NaturalNews.com. She lives in Richmond, Virginia, with her husband and their son.

Visit Hope's two Facebook pages: "Biblical Eating Resources" and "Holy Cow by Hope Egan" for more information.

CPSIA information can be obtained at www.ICGtesting.com
Printed in the USA
BVOW010101180313

315771BV00004B/19/P